A TWENTY-FIFTH ANNIVERSARY ALBUM OF NASA

BY GREGORY VOGT

FRANKLIN WATTS
NEW YORK | LONDON | TORONTO
SYDNEY | 1983

THIS BOOK IS DEDICATED
TO SOMEONE VERY SPECIAL TO ME—

MY MOTHER, HELEN VOGT.

All photographs courtesy of NASA

Library of Congress Cataloging in Publication Data

Vogt, Gregory.
A twenty-fifth anniversary album of NASA.

Bibliography: p.
Includes index.
Summary: A brief history of NASA's development,
from its early stages of research, through the
space shuttle programs, to conjectures about
future projects in space research and travel.
1. United States. National Aeronautics
and Space Administration—Juvenile literature.
2. Astronautics—United States—History—
Juvenile literature. [1. United States.
National Aeronautics and Space Administration.
2. Astronautics—History.   3. Space sciences.
4. Space flight]   I. Title.
TL521.V64 1983   629.4'0973   83-6556
ISBN 0-531-04655-9 (lib. bdg.)
ISBN 0-531-03591-3

CONTENTS

A TWENTY-FIFTH ANNIVERSARY ALBUM OF NASA

INTRODUCTION

A SIMPLE BEGINNING

December 17, 1903
Kitty Hawk, North Carolina

Success. Four flights Thursday morning. All against twenty-one mile wind. Started from level with engine power alone. Average speed through air thirty-one miles. Longest 57 seconds. Inform press. Home Christmas.   *Orville*

It was an unbelievably humble message to their father. Orville and Wilbur Wright had just achieved the first true airplane flight with a human pilot aboard. On sand dunes overlooking the Atlantic Ocean at Kill Devil Hill near Kitty Hawk, North Carolina, the two brothers had finally succeeded in getting their flimsy flying machine to take to the air. Their first flight, with Orville as pilot, traveled a pitiful 120 feet (37 m) in twelve seconds at the incredible speed of 7 miles (11.2 km) per hour into a 21-mile-per-hour (33.8-kmph) head wind. During the last of the four flights, the plane covered a distance of 582 feet (177.6 m). Strong winds eventually stopped the experimentation that day by wrecking the aircraft.

It is probable that neither Wilbur nor Orville Wright really understood the significance of what they had done that December 17. Here were two former bicycle repair shop owners taking humankind's first important steps off our planet. Others had achieved flight before—by leaping off cliffs using early forerunners of today's hang gliders or the gentle lifting force of hot air captured inside giant balloons. These flights, however, were passive, taking advantage of air currents and the buoyancy of hot air. The devices would go only where the air carried them. What

OUR ABILITY TODAY TO SEE THE EARTH FROM SPACE IS DIRECTLY LINKED WITH THE WRIGHT BROTHERS ACHIEVEMENT IN 1903.

the Wright brothers achieved was true powered flight. They had constructed a device that gave them the freedom to go where they wanted.

ROCKETS AND CABBAGES

Diary of Dr. Robert H. Goddard
March 17, 1926

The first flight with a rocket using liquid propellants was made yesterday at Aunt Effie's farm in Auburn . . . . It looked almost magical as it rose, without any appreciably greater noise or flame, as if it said, "I've been here long enough; I think I'll be going somewhere else, if you don't mind." . . . . Some of the surprising things were the absence of smoke, the lack of very loud roar, and the smallness of the flame.

Most historians believe that rockets were invented in China sometime in the eleventh century and were first used for fireworks displays and as a weapon to repel invaders. Those first rockets were probably more dangerous to the Chinese than to the invaders—they were just as likely to explode as to fly!

Regardless, rocket development continued, and throughout the centuries experimenters built bigger and more powerful rockets. In the seven hundred years following their invention, however, rockets did not change appreciably.

Then, in 1926, the first really important change in rocketry took place. A New England scientist successfully launched the world's first liquid-propellant rocket. The scientist was Robert H. Goddard. As early as 1909 Goddard had conceived of the idea of using liquid propellants for rockets, and after seventeen years of research he was ready to test his idea. His rocket used gasoline and liquid oxygen as propellants. After remaining on the ground for several seconds, the rocket climbed for two and a half seconds to a height of 41 feet (12.5 m) and then fell ingloriously into a cabbage patch 184 feet (56.1 m) away. Goddard calculated that his rocket had reached a speed of 60 miles (96 km) per hour.

Goddard continued his research and experimentation for many years. He eventually moved his test site from his Aunt Effie's farm in Auburn, Massachusetts (at the popular request of the local townspeople!), to a remote site in Rosewell, New Mexico.

Like the first flight of the Wright brothers twenty-three years earlier, Goddard's rocket flight was remarkable only in that it was the first of its kind. All the same, it was a

ABOVE: WITH ORVILLE AS PI-LOT, THE WRIGHT BROTHERS' FLYER TAKES TO THE AIR ON ITS FIRST FLIGHT. THE DATE IS DECEMBER 17, 1903.

RIGHT: ROBERT GODDARD STANDS NEXT TO THE ROCK-ET THAT IN 1926 MADE THE WORLD'S FIRST LIQUID-PROPELLANT POWERED FLIGHT.

significant step. Airplanes can operate only in the atmosphere. To get into space requires a different kind of vehicle. Goddard's rocket was the forerunner of the giant vehicles that would later carry spacecraft and astronauts into space.

THE NATIONAL AERONAUTICS AND SPACE ADMINISTRATION

On the first day of October 1958, a new agency of the U.S. government came into being. For nearly a year, the leaders, lawmakers, and people of the United States had been locked into a kind of hysteria. On October 4, 1957, the Soviet Union astounded the world by launching the world's first artificial satellite. A "red star" was orbiting the earth. From the moment the Russians announced their achievement, a new word—*Sputnik*—became a part of nearly everyone's vocabulary.

Sputnik was a 184-pound (83.6-kg) metal ball, with four spikelike antennae that beeped electronic signals back to earth. *Sputnik*, the word itself, literally meant "traveling companion," but to Americans it meant that the Soviet Union was ahead of the United States in space technology. If the Soviets could launch satellites, they could also launch bombs. From the White House, the halls of Congress, and the homes of most Americans came a demand to *do* something. The United States must catch up with the Russians in space technology.

Actually, the United States was not far behind in satellite-launching capabilities, and in some other areas of space research it was actually ahead. It just *seemed* that we were far behind because overhead was *Sputnik*.

FORGOTTEN "TOYS"

Ironically, though both the airplane and the liquid-propellant rocket were invented in the United States, they were both also largely ignored by Americans in the early years. An interest in airplanes developed in Europe, however, after the Wright brothers made a number of demonstration flights there. When World War I broke out, Europeans quickly recognized the airplane to be an important vehicle for war. As the United States drew ever closer to direct involvement in the conflict, it became clear that there was a serious deficiency in American aeronautical knowledge. Something had to be done to catch up.

In 1915 Congress passed a new law creating a panel of scientists to promote aeronautical development in the United States. The panel was called the National Advisory

Committee on Aeronautics, and it opened for business later that year. NACA, as it was usually called, opened an aeronautical laboratory near Hampton, Virginia. Wind tunnels were constructed, and studies on all phases of flight began. NACA continued for many years, and, by the time the United States entered World War II, two more research facilities had been opened, in Ohio and California. It was NACA that would eventually form the core of NASA in 1958.

VERGELTUNGSWAFFE (V-2)

During World War II a devastating new weapon was developed by the Third Reich of Germany. This was the V-2 missile. The V-2 was a liquid-propellant rocket standing almost 46 feet (14 m) tall. Using 19,300 pounds (8,773 kg) of alcohol and liquid oxygen as propellants, the V-2 could launch a 2,150-pound (977-kg) explosive warhead on a high arcing trajectory that could carry it up to 200 miles (320 km)—right into the heart of London.

The V-2 seemed an invincible weapon. Once launched, nothing could be done to stop it. It would fall silently, without warning, and could wipe out whole city blocks.

The V-2 was the result of a major commitment on the part of the Third Reich. Thousands of Germans worked to develop and mass produce the weapons. Though developed independently from Robert Goddard's rockets, the V-2 was remarkably similar to the advanced liquid-propellant rockets Goddard had developed with his tiny crew of workers in the New Mexican desert. Goddard's work, however, had been largely ignored in the United States.

AEROSPACE RESEARCH
BEGINS IN EARNEST

In the late 1940s and early 1950s, the United States became actively involved in both aeronautical and rocket research. The National Advisory Committee on Aeronautics had proved itself invaluable in the development of advanced aircraft for military and civilian use. Rocket research had been spurred on by the war.

At the close of World War II, Allied forces advanced on Germany from both the East and West. The scientists of the German rocket team, headed by Dr. Wernher von Braun, decided to surrender in order to preserve the advances they had made in the science of rocketry. A disagreement arose among team members, however, and some of the team, plus many of the rocket technicians, chose to surrender to the Soviet forces. Von Braun and

DR. WERNHER VON BRAUN (SEATED ON TABLE) POSES IN 1956 WITH OFFICIALS OF THE ARMY BALLISTIC MISSILE AGENCY AT HUNTSVILLE, ALABAMA. CLOCKWISE, STARTING WITH VON BRAUN, ARE HERMANN OBERTH, DR. ERNST STUBLINGER, MAJ. GEN. H.N. TOFTOY, AND DR. EBERHARD REES.

many of his top aides, meanwhile, chose to surrender to the U.S. forces. In addition, a number of unused V-2 missiles were captured by the United States. At the end of the war, von Braun, his team, and the captured V-2s were brought to the United States. The von Braun team finally settled at the Redstone Arsenal near Huntsville, Alabama, where they would form the core of America's rocket research program.

Experiments with V-2 rockets under the code name "Operation Paperclip" gave the newly formed missile-development teams valuable experience in liquid-propellant rocketry. During one 1949 experiment, ("Bumper WAC"), a WAC Corporal rocket was mounted on top of a V-2 and launched as a two-stage rocket. The WAC Corporal broke all altitude records when it climbed to a height of more than 250 miles (403 km).

THE RACE WAS ON

The United States was just a few months away from launching its own first satellite when news came of *Sputnik*'s successful launch. A variety of U.S. rockets, such as the Viking, Nike, Aerobee, and Redstone, had already been tested, and a new Atlas was nearing completion. Unfortunately, a rivalry between different branches of the military, to see who could get the official "go ahead" first, delayed the entire project, giving the Soviets the chance to send their satellite into space first.

The job of handling the first U.S. satellite launch was at last awarded to the Navy, and on December 6, 1957, *Vanguard 1*, with a tiny satellite aboard, stood poised on the launchpad. In front of a small army of newspeople, *Vanguard* barely raised itself, broke into pieces, then disintegrated entirely in an exploding ball of flame. After that humiliation, the job of launching the first U.S. satellite was turned over to the von Braun rocket team, which was operating under the auspices of the Army. Von Braun promised to put a satellite up within ninety days. On January 31, 1958, well within the specified ninety-day period, *Explorer 1* was launched into orbit on a Jupiter C rocket. America was at last in space.

Not only was *Explorer 1* America's first satellite, it was also the first to make a really important discovery in space. With instruments placed inside by the astrophysicist James Van Allen, *Explorer 1* discovered a ring of trapped solar particles encircling the earth. The existence of this radioactive ring was later confirmed with additional satellite launches, and a second ring was discovered. In honor of the scientist, the rings were named the Van Allen Radiation Belts.

ABOVE: BUMPER WAC LIFTS OFF IN 1949 USING A GERMAN V-2 ROCKET FOR THE FIRST STAGE AND AN ARMY WAC CORPORAL ROCKET FOR THE SECOND STAGE.

RIGHT: AMERICA'S HOPES FOR ITS FIRST SATELLITE LAUNCH EXPLODE ON THE LAUNCH-PAD WITH *VANGUARD 1.*

ABOVE: ONE OF THE VAN-GUARD SATELLITES UNDER-GOES A CHECKUP BEFORE BE-ING LAUNCHED INTO SPACE.

RIGHT: A JUPITER C ROCKET CONTAINING *EXPLORER 1* IS SHOWN HERE IN THE FINAL STAGES OF PREPARATION BE-FORE ITS JANUARY 31, 1958, LAUNCH.

NASA, THE EARLY YEARS

1

While the U.S. space program was just getting itself organized, the Soviets added to America's feeling of inferiority by launching an 11-pound (5-kg) black and white dog named Kudryavka ("Little Curly") on board a 1,120-pound (509-kg) satellite just one month after *Sputnik 1*. The dog, which came to be known around the world by its breed name, Laika, later died in orbit when its oxygen ran out. Following this, on May 15, 1958, the Soviets launched into orbit a 2,925-pound (1,330-kg) science laboratory.

The weights of the Soviet satellites were astounding. The best that the United States had been able to achieve was the 31-pound (14.1-kg) *Explorer 3*. *Vanguard* had weighed only 3¼ pounds (1.7 kg). Soviet Premier Nikita Khrushchev had scoffed at the light satellite, calling it "an orange."

It became painfully obvious at that time that a coordinated space effort was needed. On July 29, 1958, President Dwight D. Eisenhower signed the National Aeronautics and Space Act that created the National Aeronautics and Space Administration (NASA). It had been decided that the best way to counter the image of Soviet superiority in space technology would be to have a publicly open space program, run by a civilian space agency. All space activities, in other words, both successful and unsuccessful, would be reported to the public. Openness would be one of the chief features of America's space effort. In the Space Act, NASA's objective was clearly stated: "To explore the phenomenon of the atmosphere and space for peaceful purposes for the benefit of all mankind." The new agency was to begin operations on October 1, 1958.

The job of running NASA was given to T. Keith Glennan, then president of the Case Institute of Technology. It was a monumental task. However, Glennan would be assisted by NACA and its director, Hugh L. Dryden, who would become NASA's deputy administrator. NACA would be abolished, but its laboratories would form the heart of the new agency. Glennan would have to bring together NACA personnel, military rocket personnel, and a host of civilian space scientists in a coordinated effort to overtake the Soviets in the race for space.

The early years at NASA were very exciting. The race with the Soviet Union was on. For a while, it appeared that the Soviets were winning. One failed U.S. launch followed another. The results were sometimes spectacular. Rockets would teeter on the launchpad, only to flop over and erupt into flames. The Soviets had their failures, too, but they weren't talking about them.

On April 12, 1961, another blow to America's ego came with the launch of the first human astronaut into space. Cosmonaut Major Yuri A. Gagarin rode *Vostok 1* into space and completed one orbit of earth. The first artificial satellite, the first animal in orbit, and now the first human—all were Soviet achievements.

The first American astronaut, Alan B. Shepard, Jr., made a brief trip into space during a suborbital flight on May 5, 1961. It was little to brag about. Shepard's fifteen-minute flight in a Mercury capsule carried him on a ballistic path and plopped him in the Atlantic Ocean 302 miles (486.2 km) from the launch site. He was followed into space by Virgil I. "Gus" Grissom on July 21, 1961, on a flight that was a virtual repeat of Shepard's except that Grissom's capsule sank in the Atlantic Ocean while the astronaut was being hoisted into a recovery aircraft.

On August 6, 1961, cosmonaut Gherman Titov flew a seventeen-orbit mission aboard *Vostok 2*. It was not until February 20, 1962, that the first American orbital flight would take place. Though not as impressive as Titov's flight, Lt. Col. John H. Glenn circled the earth three times in the *Friendship 7* Mercury capsule. It was clear that the Americans were beginning to "catch up" in the race for space.

THE ROAD TO MERCURY

Getting Glenn and his Mercury capsule into space had been no simple matter. Before a human could be subjected to the hazards of spaceflight, the capsule had to be tested under actual flight conditions. The job for that fell to a chimpanzee named Ham.

As early as 1948, the United States had been using monkeys for rocket research. Tests continued for many years, and on May 28, 1958, a rhesus monkey named Able and a

squirrel monkey named Baker were rocketed to speeds of 10,000 miles (16,000 km) per hour on a Jupiter C missile and recovered safely from the ocean.

Two months before Ham was scheduled to lift off, public confidence in the U.S. space effort had reached a new low. The scene was Cape Canaveral, Florida, and standing on the launchpad was a Redstone rocket with a Mercury capsule on top of it. NASA was particularly anxious for a successful launch, to demonstrate that America was truly catching up to the Soviet Union. At precisely 9 a.m. on November 21, 1960, the Redstone was fired, producing a thunderous roar. Then, as suddenly as it had started, the engine shut down, and the rocket settled back on its pedestal, after at most a 5-inch (12.7-cm) liftoff. But that wasn't the end of it. Much to the horror of the observers, the Mercury escape rocket system then fired. The orange escape tower tore loose and landed 400 yards (360 m) away, and three seconds later the drogue parachute package shot upward. This was followed by the main and reserve parachutes. As the smoke cleared, the embarrassed engineers could see the parachutes and shroud lines draping down the side of the vehicle. The cause of the catastrophe was a ground electrical disconnect plug that had pulled out at an improper angle at the moment of liftoff, causing the shutdown sequence to begin. It was a simple problem to fix, but the incident was very embarrassing to all concerned.

When it came time for Ham to fly into space, the chimp was strapped into a Mercury capsule and placed on top of a Redstone rocket. This was the same combination that would be used for human astronauts. Ham's January 31, 1961, flight lasted sixteen and a half minutes. During the flight, a thrust control became stuck, extending the splashdown point more than 120 miles (193 km) beyond the planned target. Ham had to bob around in the ocean in his capsule for several hours before he could be picked up.

Shepard's and Grissom's Mercury flights were followed by the launch of another chimpanzee—Enos. Neither astronaut had actually gone into orbit, like the Russian cosmonauts Gagarin and Titov had. Enos pioneered the way on a mission that lasted for two orbits before safe recovery from the ocean.

Enos was not just a passenger during his mission in space. He had many lever-pulling tasks to perform on cue from Mission Control. His rewards for performing these tasks correctly were banana pellets. If Enos pulled a wrong lever, he received a mild electrical shock to the soles of his feet. Due to a circuitry malfunction, Enos

LEFT: ALAN B. SHEPARD, JR., PILOTS A MERCURY CAPSULE ON AMERICA'S FIRST MANNED SUBORBITAL FLIGHT OF MAY 5, 1961.

RIGHT: SHEPARD BEING RE-COVERED BY HELICOPTER FROM THE ATLANTIC OCEAN.

ABOVE: THE SEVEN MERCURY
ASTRONAUTS POSE DURING
SURVIVAL TRAINING IN NE-
VADA. FROM LEFT TO RIGHT:
GORDON COOPER, SCOTT
CARPENTER, JOHN GLENN,
ALAN SHEPARD, VIRGIL GRIS-
SOM, WALTER SCHIRRA, AND
DONALD ("DEKE") SLAYTON.

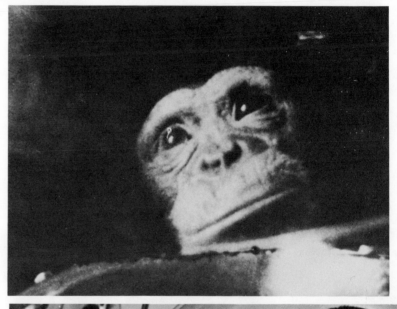

LEFT: AN EMBARRASSING
ATTEMPT TO LAUNCH A MER-
CURY-REDSTONE ROCKET
ON NOVEMBER 21, 1960, IS
SHOWN IN THIS SEQUENCE
OF PHOTOGRAPHS. THE ES-
CAPE TOWER BLASTS AWAY
FROM THE CAPSULE AND
PARACHUTES DEPLOY AS
THE ROCKET SETTLES BACK
ON THE LAUNCHPAD.

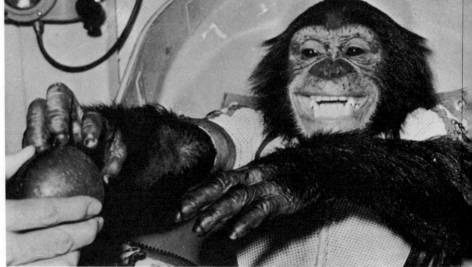

RIGHT: HAM, THE FIRST CHIM-
PANZEE TO FLY IN SPACE,
GRIMACES DURING HIS 5,000-
MILE (8,050-KM) RIDE IN A
MERCURY CAPSULE AND
REACHES FOR FOOD FROM A
CREWMAN ON THE U.S.S.
DONNER FOLLOWING THE
RIDE.

sometimes received shocks when he should have received pellets. Nevertheless, he continued faithfully pulling levers, hoping to get more pellets. Enos demonstrated that human astronauts would be able to perform a variety of manual tasks while in orbit around the earth.

John Glenn's flight, though successful, was also not without problems. Nearing the California coastline on the first orbit, Glenn's capsule became unstable, and Glenn found it necessary to shut down the automatic control system and use manual control for the rest of the flight.

Even more serious was a signal received at Mission Control indicating that the capsule's heat shield and landing bag were no longer in place. If this were so, Glenn and his capsule might both burn up during atmospheric reentry. After Glenn's safe return, it was discovered that the problem had really been with one of the ground receivers, and that the trouble signal had been a false one.

FAR LEFT: FRIENDSHIP 7, WITH JOHN GLENN ON BOARD, BEGINS A 17,500-MPH (28,175-KMPH), THREE-ORBIT RIDE ON TOP OF AN ATLAS 6 ROCKET.

LEFT: GLENN EXPERIENCES WEIGHTLESSNESS DURING HIS FLIGHT AROUND THE EARTH. LATER HIS SPACECRAFT IS BROUGHT ALONGSIDE THE RECOVERY SHIP.

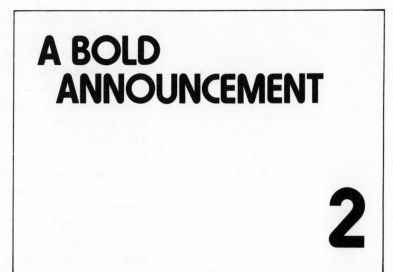

A BOLD ANNOUNCEMENT

2

Twenty days after Alan Shepard's Mercury flight, President John F. Kennedy startled the world with an address made before a joint session of Congress.

"I believe that this nation should commit itself to achieving the goal, before this decade is out, of landing a man on the moon and returning him safely to earth. No single space program in this period will be more impressive to mankind or more important to the long-range exploration of space; and none so difficult or expensive to accomplish."

The plan to go to the moon was an ambitious one, to say the least. But to pledge to do it after just one fifteen-minute suborbital flight and within ten years seemed like a wild boast. Yet Kennedy was backed by the Congress and the American people.

HOW TO DO IT

Kennedy's commitment to go to the moon wasn't exactly a wild idea. When NASA inherited the research facilities and personnel at the Redstone Arsenal in Alabama, to form what is today the Marshall Space Flight Center, it also inherited plans for a superbooster, the Saturn rocket. It was Saturn V rockets that would eventually be pressed into service for the moon missions.

The major decision to be made was how best to travel to the moon and back. Scientists came up with three possible methods. The first was an earth-orbit rendezvous. With this approach, various pieces of the spacecraft would be carried into orbit on separate rockets and then joined together in space before making the trip to the moon. The second approach was a direct ascent approach, in which the entire spacecraft would be launched from the surface of the earth and go directly to the moon. The third approach was a lunar-orbit rendezvous. In this plan, the complete spacecraft would be launched into orbit around the moon, and then a portion of the spacecraft would make the actual descent while the "mother" ship remained in lunar orbit.

In June 1962, the lunar-orbit rendezvous approach was decided upon. It would be safer and less expensive than the other two options. The spacecraft would have three modules. During the trip to the moon and back, three astronauts would ride in a cone-shaped command module. This would be attached to a service module, which would serve as an upper rocket stage for propulsion and would provide electrical power. Until reentry, the command and service modules would remain as a single unit. The third module would be a four-legged lander that would carry two astronauts to the surface of the moon. The upper portion of this module would serve as an ascent rocket for launch from the moon. After its rendezvous in lunar orbit with the mother ship, the ascent stage would be left behind, and the astronauts would return to earth in the command and service modules.

GEMINI

By the completion of the sixth Mercury flight, in May 1963, NASA had gained important experience in launching spacecraft into orbit, controlling them while in flight, and returning them from space. The next step was to upgrade the spacecraft itself by making room for a second astronaut on board. The new spacecraft, called Gemini, a name meaning "twins," was almost three times the size and weight of the Mercury capsule. Another important lesson NASA had learned from the Mercury flights was that it was not necessary to have all systems inside the capsule. Much equipment could be placed outside and left behind on reentry.

The first manned Gemini flight, *Gemini 3*, took place on March 23, 1965. It was only a brief, three-orbit flight for Gus Grissom and John W. Young, but it demonstrated the feasibility of the Gemini capsule design. *Gemini 3* was quickly followed by *Gemini 4*, and a spectacular walk in space by astronaut Edward H. White, II. To go outside, White donned a new kind of flight suit. On Mercury missions, the flight suits worn by the astronauts had simply been pressure suits, designed to act as backups if the cabin lost its pressure. With Gemini, the suits were designed not only to provide backup pressure, but also to protect the crew members in the vacuum of space and from the wide range of temperatures encountered there.

White's spacewalk lasted twenty minutes. Though

White was attached to the space capsule by an "umbilical cord," he had great freedom to float and tumble as he wished. Part of the time he was outside, he experimented with a handheld propulsion unit—basically a gun with two small tanks of compressed oxygen. Pulling the trigger released propulsive jets of gas, which could be used to move White around. White enjoyed his spacewalk so much he was reluctant to end it.

Walking in space was one of the important experiments that had to be conducted before astronauts could travel to the moon. Other experiments included practicing rendezvous maneuvers between two spacecraft and spacecraft docking. Both these activities were planned to take place during the lunar-orbit rendezvous mission.

The first spacecraft rendezvous attempt between two manned spacecraft came with the launch of *Gemini 7* on December 4, 1965. Eleven days later, *Gemini 6* was launched, and the two spacecraft maneuvered to within a few feet (0.6 m) of each other. (*Gemini 6* returned to earth two days before *Gemini 7;* hence the lower mission number.)

The *Gemini 8* mission that took place the following March registered another first for the American space program. Neil A. Armstrong and David Scott docked and latched their Gemini spacecraft with an Agena target vehicle.

While the two craft were still docked, however, trouble broke out with a thruster. Both vehicles began to roll violently. Armstrong immediately took control and undocked *Gemini 8* from its target. To stop the rolling, he found it necessary to resort to his reentry control system. Having thus used this system, he had to return to earth as quickly as possible.

The Gemini program came to an end with the flight of *Gemini 12* in November 1966. During the ten manned flights, NASA astronauts had accumulated nearly thirteen hours of extravehicular activity, accomplished several rendezvous with unmanned and manned target vehicles, and completed several dockings, including one where the target's rocket was used to propel the combined vehicle into a new orbit. It seemed as if America was ready to go to the moon.

MORE SOVIET FIRSTS

While NASA was gearing up for the Gemini flights, the Soviets scored several more firsts. On June 16, 1963, Valentina Tereshkova, a textile factory worker, became the first woman to fly into space. Tereshkova's flight served

ABOVE LEFT: GEMINI 3, WITH VIRGIL GRISSOM AND JOHN YOUNG ON BOARD, LIFTS OFF INTO SPACE ON TOP OF A TITAN LAUNCH VEHICLE.

ABOVE RIGHT: ASTRONAUT ED WHITE, ATTACHED TO *GEMINI 4* BY A TETHER, DRIFTS IN SPACE ON HIS HISTORIC SPACEWALK.

BELOW LEFT: GEMINI 6 WAS PHOTOGRAPHED BY THE CREW OF *GEMINI 7* DURING A RENDEZVOUS BETWEEN THE TWO SPACECRAFT ON DECEMBER 15, 1965.

BELOW RIGHT: THE AGENA TARGET DOCKING VEHICLE AS SEEN FROM *GEMINI 8.*

no real technical or scientific purpose, but it did give the Soviets the chance to claim that their space technology was so advanced that even an average citizen could participate in the program. It would be nearly twenty years before the next female cosmonaut would have the opportunity to go into space.

Another first was the launch of a three-man Voskhod space capsule. It was the first multimanned mission in space. Soviet newspapers mocked the U.S. with the headlines "SORRY, APOLLO." (It would still be a number of years before the first manned Apollo would fly.)

The most important "first" was the spacewalk of Lt. Col. Alexsei Leonov, during the one-day *Voskhod 2* flight on March 18, 1965. The Russian flight beat the first Gemini flight by five days and Ed White's spacewalk by ten weeks.

Though the Soviets bragged about the spacewalk, Leonov and his mate Pavel Belyayev courted disaster no less than three times during the mission. Because of the stiffness of his space suit, Leonov had great difficulty reentering his capsule. Later, the capsule's autopilot system failed, and manual landing procedures had to be employed. When the two cosmonauts looked out of their capsule after landing, they found themselves in a snowy forest in the Russian Ural Mountains 2,000 miles (3,220 km) off course. The two spent a cold night in the capsule, with hungry wolves prowling outside, before rescue teams could arrive the next morning.

For two years following the spacewalk mission, the Soviet press was strangely quiet about its country's space program. The next cosmonaut would not fly until April 1967.

TRAGEDY

With the obvious success of the Gemini program, the moon seemed very near. While the Gemini capsules were flying, NASA conducted tests on the Saturn launch vehicles that would carry the Apollo capsules and the lunar module. In addition, a very successful unmanned lunar exploration program was already underway. Three Ranger television spacecraft had made hard landings on the moon and revealed areas on the lunar surface that seemed smooth enough for lunar modules to land. These were followed by a string of soft-landing Surveyors, which photographed the landscape and studied the quality and composition of the soil. The Surveyors provided evidence that the moon's surface was firm enough to support landers and would not "swallow them in pools of dust." Along

ABOVE LEFT: JUST 2.3 SECONDS BEFORE IMPACT, *RANGER 7* TOOK THIS PICTURE OF THE MOON. AT THE TIME THE PICTURE WAS TAKEN, *RANGER 7* WAS JUST 3 MILES (4.8 KM) ABOVE THE MOON.

ABOVE RIGHT: A MOSAIC OF THE MOON'S SURFACE TAKEN BY *SURVEYOR 7.*

BELOW: EARTHRISE OVER THE MOON AS SEEN BY *LUNAR ORBITER 1* ON AUGUST 23, 1966.

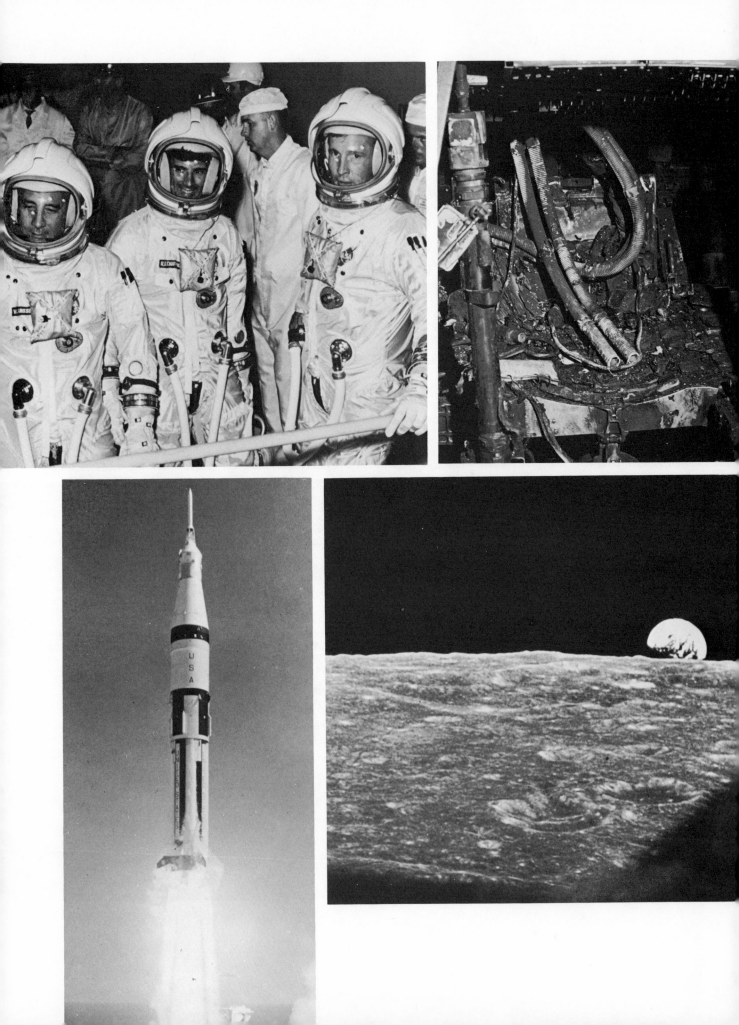

with the Surveyors came the "flying drugstores," or the lunar orbiters. They were called this because they developed their own film and scanned the pictures before sending them back to earth by radio transmission. The photographs were useful in mapping much of the surface of the moon and in selecting suitable landing sites for the Apollo missions.

Back on earth, three astronauts, Gus Grissom, Ed White, and Roger Chaffee, were selected for the first of the manned Apollo test flights. On January 27, 1967, the three were going through a routine rehearsal of their upcoming flight, and were wearing space suits and sitting inside their capsule atop a Saturn rocket, when Chaffee reported a fire. The astronauts tried to release the hatch and scramble out, but the heat and smoke built up so rapidly that they were overcome by it before they could escape. In moments, the three were dead.

The exact cause of the tragedy was never determined, but it was generally thought that a spark, perhaps caused by a short circuit, started the blaze. An investigating board later pointed to a number of problems in the capsule's design. The inside contained many nonmetallic flammable objects, such as wiring insulation, Velcro patches, and paper checklists. In flight, the capsule atmosphere would be pure oxygen, at a pressure of 5 pounds per square inch (5 psi); in that environment, objects burn quite normally. But on the launchpad the atmosphere was pure oxygen at 16 psi. Under those conditions, objects burn explosively. Furthermore, the inward opening hatch was hard to operate and took too much time to release. These and a number of other design problems contributed to the tragedy.

BACK ON TRACK

It took twenty-two months of soul-searching and many spacecraft design changes, but the Apollo program at last got back on course for the moon. On October 11, 1968, the eleven-day *Apollo 7* flight began. Inside the capsule were Walter Schirra, Donn Eisele, and Walter Cunningham. During the successful earth-orbital flight, eight firings of the service module engine took place, and the astronauts rendezvoused to within 70 feet (23 m) of the upper stage of their launch rocket.

A few months later, on December 21, a truly spectacular spaceflight began. *Apollo 8* rode into orbit on the first Saturn V rocket used to carry astronauts into space. After a short time in orbit, Frank Borman, James Lovell, and William Anders blasted out of orbit and headed for the moon.

ABOVE LEFT: ASTRONAUTS VIRGIL GRISSOM (*LEFT*), ROGER CHAFFEE, AND ED WHITE POSE IN THEIR FLIGHT SUITS JUST A FEW MONTHS BEFORE THE CAPSULE FIRE THAT TRAGICALLY ENDED THEIR LIVES.

ABOVE RIGHT: THE INTERIOR OF THE APOLLO CAPSULE FOLLOWING THE FIRE THAT KILLED ASTRONAUTS CHAFFEE, GRISSOM, AND WHITE.

BELOW LEFT: A SATURN IB LAUNCH VEHICLE CARRIES *APOLLO 7* INTO SPACE.

BELOW RIGHT: EARTHRISE OVER THE MOON AS SEEN BY THE *APOLLO 8* CREW FROM THEIR SPACECRAFT.

Once there, the crew circled the moon ten times, transmitted a Christmas Eve message to all people on earth, and took superb pictures of the moon's surface.

In March and May of 1969, two more important steps were taken, with *Apollo 9* and *Apollo 10*. *Apollo 9*, in earth orbit, tested all the spacecraft parts that would be used to land on the lunar surface. The lunar module separated from the command and service modules and executed rendezvous and docking procedures. *Apollo 10* carried the practice much further, by taking the lander to within 10 miles (16 km) of the moon's surface before returning to the mother ship and then earth.

"ONE SMALL STEP"

3

At 9:32 a.m., eastern daylight time, on July 16, 1969, a 3,250-ton rocket, 60 feet (19.7 m) taller than the Statue of Liberty, roared into action. With a thrust of 7½ million pounds (33.6 million newtons), *Apollo 11* began its journey to the moon. Leaving earth orbit at a speed of more than 24,000 miles (38,640 km) per hour, *Apollo 11* reached the moon in just three days. On arriving there, the service module engine slowed the craft and put Neil Armstrong, Edward ("Buzz") Aldrin, Jr., and Mike Collins into lunar orbit.

After circling the moon eleven times, Armstrong and Aldrin crawled through the tunnel leading to the lunar module and checked out its systems. They then undocked the craft, leaving Collins behind.

Piloting perhaps the strangest flying contraption ever constructed, Armstrong fired the descent engine to bring the lander out of orbit. For a while the lander, named the *Eagle*, remained in a horizontal position relative to the moon. But as it lost altitude and approached the surface, it turned to assume a vertical position.

At 500 feet (150 m) above the surface, Armstrong took over the controls. The automated landing system was bringing the *Eagle* down into a boulder-filled crater. Armstrong applied lateral thrust and moved the *Eagle* to a safer site. Following touchdown, Armstrong calmly announced: "Houston, Tranquility Base here. The *Eagle* has landed."

Nine hours after landing in the lunar Sea of Tranquility, the hatch opened and Armstrong started down the ladder. Before a television audience of an estimated 500 million or more, Armstrong paused on the bottom step of the ladder. When he finally stepped off he said: "That's one small step for [a] man . . . one giant leap for mankind."

[28]

RIGHT: NEIL ARMSTRONG LEADS MIKE COLLINS AND BUZZ ALDRIN INTO THE VAN THAT WILL TRANSPORT THEM TO THE LAUNCHPAD FOR THE LIFTOFF OF *APOLLO 11.*

BELOW LEFT: APOLLO 11 LIFTS OFF AT 9:32 A.M., EASTERN DAYLIGHT TIME, FROM LAUNCH COMPLEX 39A AT THE KENNEDY SPACE CENTER.

BELOW RIGHT: FOOTPRINT ON THE MOON LEFT BY THE *APOLLO 11* ASTRONAUTS.

OPP. TOP LEFT: BUZZ ALDRIN IS SEEN HERE COMING DOWN THE LADDER OF THE *EAGLE* LANDER DURING THE *APOLLO 11* MISSION.

OPP. TOP RIGHT: ALDRIN STANDS NEXT TO AN AMERICAN FLAG PLANTED ON THE MOON'S SURFACE DURING THE APOLLO 11 MISSION.

OPP. BOTTOM LEFT: BY CHANCE, ALL PHOTOGRAPHS TAKEN ON THE MOON'S SURFACE DURING *APOLLO 11* SHOW ASTRONAUT BUZZ ALDRIN. NEIL ARMSTRONG HELD THE CAMERA, BUT IN THIS PHOTOGRAPH HIS REFLECTION APPEARED ON ALDRIN'S VISOR.

OPP. BOTTOM RIGHT: THE ASCENT STAGE OF THE *APOLLO 11* LUNAR MODULE IS MAKING ITS APPROACH TO THE COMMAND AND SERVICE MODULES FOLLOWING ITS HISTORIC LANDING ON THE MOON.

Though the United States had just won the race for the moon, the event meant much more than that. In all of human history, no one had ever set foot on the surface of another body in space. For a time, people around the world were filled with awe and proud at what humans could achieve. It was not just America's but everybody's victory.

Nineteen minutes after Armstrong stepped onto the surface of the moon, Aldrin followed. For two hours, the two performed scientific investigations together and gathered 44 pounds (20 kg) of rock and dirt to bring home. Honoring the nation that sent them, they erected an American flag.

About twelve hours after the first moon walk ended, Armstrong and Aldrin were blasted back into orbit by the ascent stage of the lander to join Collins. The first manned moon mission ended with a splashdown in the Pacific Ocean on July 24.

APOLLO 12

The moon landings continued in November 1969 with *Apollo 12*. Demonstrating "pinpoint" navigation, *Apollo 12* landed within 600 feet (197 m) of the *Surveyor III* robot spacecraft that had landed there two and a half years before. Astronauts Alan L. Bean and Richard F. Gordon, Jr., spent a total of fifteen and a half hours collecting 75 pounds (34.1 kg) of samples and deploying automated science experiments that would continue to operate even after they left.

"HOUSTON, WE'VE HAD A PROBLEM HERE"

A more ambitious mission was planned for the next flight. Jim Lovell, who circled the moon in *Apollo 8*, would get his chance to walk on the moon. Riding with Lovell were Fred W. Haise, Jr., and John L. Swigert, Jr. Swigert was assigned to the flight at the eleventh hour, when it was learned that Ken Mattingly, the original command module pilot, had been exposed to German measles. The current NASA administrator decided to play it safe and keep Mattingly on the ground. (Mattingly never did come down with the measles.)

The *Apollo 13* flight began with a normal liftoff on April 11, 1970. In spite of a few minor problems, the flight seemed to be the smoothest yet. Joe Kerwin, the capcom (capsule communicator), complained, "We're bored to tears down here." That mood would soon change.

ABOVE: A FISH-EYE CAMERA LENS VIEW OF THE INTERIOR OF THE *APOLLO 12* CAPSULE, WITH ALAN BEAN (*LEFT*), RICHARD GORDON, AND CHARLES CONRAD.

BELOW: ASTRONAUT ALAN BEAN STANDS NEXT TO THE *SURVEYOR 3* SPACECRAFT ON THE MOON.

Just a few minutes following a live television broadcast to earth, during which the crew explained how easily one could adapt to living and working in space, disaster struck. The crew heard a sharp bang and felt vibrations. A warning light flashed, and Swigert radioed, "Houston, we've had a problem here." His calm message was an understatement. It took many minutes before the magnitude of the situation was realized. Unknown to the crew and flight controllers, an oxygen tank in the service module had blown up. Additional warning lights indicated that two of three electricity-producing fuel cells had failed. (The fuel cells use oxygen and hydrogen to produce electricity.) Furthermore, another oxygen tank was leaking. When that tank was empty, the last fuel cell would die, and the service module would become a useless hulk.

Had *Apollo 13* been in earth orbit, the return would have been relatively simple, but the ship was 200,000 miles (322,000 km) from earth and headed toward the moon. It would have to use the moon's gravity and the thrust from the lander to get back home. The lunar module would also have to serve as home for the crew for the next few days. Designed to be used by two people for forty-five hours, the module would have to be used by three people for ninety hours. Fred Haise, an expert in lunar module design, calculated that the remaining oxygen supplies would be sufficient for the astronauts to reach home safely, but battery power and water supplies for cooling and drinking would run short. Every unnecessary electrical device was turned off, and each crew member was allowed only 6 ounces (177 ml) of drinking water per day. There were enough lithium hydroxide canisters in the command module to cleanse carbon dioxide from the air, but the square canisters of the command module would not fit the round holes in the lunar module. Some tape, plastic bags, and cardboard eventually solved the attachment problem.

During the long hours of the return home, sleep was almost impossible. By turning down the power, the crew lost their heat. The cabin temperature dropped to 38°F (3°C). Water condensed in droplets on all surfaces and frosted over the windows. Food was refrigerator cold.

Six days after the flight began, the command module of *Apollo 13* shucked the service module and the lander that had served as a lifeboat, and streaked back into the atmosphere for a splashdown in the Pacific Ocean. *Apollo 13* was a failure only in the technical sense. The crew was safe, and everyone breathed a sigh of relief.

ABOVE: JUST BEFORE REENTRY, THE CREW OF *APOLLO 13* SNAPPED THIS PICTURE OF THE SEVERELY DAMAGED SERVICE MODULE.

BELOW: BREATHING A SIGH OF RELIEF, THE CREWMEN OF *APOLLO 13*, FRED HAISE (*LEFT*), JAMES LOVELL, AND JOHN SWIGERT, STEP DOWN FROM THE HELICOPTER TO THE DECK OF THE RECOVERY SHIP.

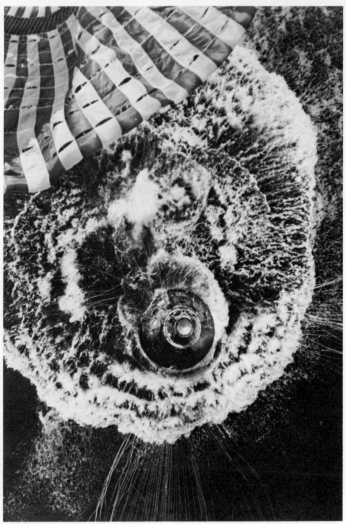

PUBLIC INTEREST FADES

Nine months following *Apollo 13*, the flights resumed. Between January 31, 1971, and December 19, 1972, four more landings on the moon took place. With each mission, the number of hours of moon walking grew. During *Apollo 17*, the moon walkers made three jaunts on the lunar surface, for a total time of twenty-two hours, and collected 243 pounds (110.45 kg) of samples.

Starting with *Apollo 15*, moving around on the moon was made easier with the addition of the first extraterrestrial car, the Lunar Rover. The four-wheel, two-seater car was unfolded from the side of the lander. Each wheel was powered by a ¼ horsepower electric motor. On a straightaway and with two astronauts inside, it could hit 7 mph (11.2 kmph). During the last mission, speed records were smashed when the rover topped 11 mph (17.7 kmph) going downhill.

By the conclusion of the Apollo expeditions, most previous information about the moon had been rendered obsolete. A total of 843 pounds (383.2 kg) of rocks and soil had been collected, thousands of photographs had been taken, and many scientific instruments and experiments had been placed and then left, still running, on the moon's surface.

In spite of the great success of the program, however, many people became bored with it. "What's in it for me?" they asked. Some people even went so far as to call their local TV stations to complain that live coverage of the moon walks was interfering with reruns of their favorite TV shows.

ABOVE: ASTRONAUT JAMES IRWIN IS SEEN HERE STANDING BETWEEN THE LANDER AND THE LUNAR ROVER DURING THE *APOLLO 15* MOON MISSION.

BELOW LEFT: ASTRONAUT EUGENE CERNAN TAKES A SHORT TEST RIDE ON THE LUNAR ROVER DURING THE *APOLLO 17* MISSION ON THE MOON.

BELOW RIGHT: APOLLO 17 SPLASHES DOWN IN THE PACIFIC OCEAN ON DECEMBER 19, 1972.

SPACE STATION ONE

4

By the end of the Apollo moon missions, the longest any American astronaut had stayed in space was fourteen days. What would happen to the astronauts if they attempted to stay in space much longer, say months or years? Could they survive in good health? These were just some of the questions NASA hoped to answer when it launched America's first space station, *Skylab*.

The Skylab program took advantage of existing space-launch hardware by modifying the third stage of a Saturn V rocket to become an orbital workshop for crews of three astronauts to live and work in space for extended periods. The new station offered a whopping 13,000 cubic feet (390 cu m) of interior space.

The launch of *Skylab* took place on May 14, 1973. At first, everything seemed fine, but then, about one minute into the flight, a heat and micrometeoroid shield along the side of the workshop was ripped away by the rushing air. Moments later, two large solar panels began to deploy, and one was torn off. The second panel was blocked by a piece of metal and held in a partially opened position. Radio signals from the workshop confirmed ground controllers' suspicions of trouble. *Skylab* was producing only a fraction of its planned electrical output. (It had four additional panels.) It was overheating, too, because the missing micrometeoroid shield also served as thermal protection.

After several days of brainstorming and testing in underwater simulation tanks, repair strategies were devised. *Skylab* could be saved. On May 25, a Saturn 1B rocket was launched with the first *Skylab* crew inside. After docking with the workshop, the astronauts drifted through a tunnel to the inside. Their first order of business was to cool the station by erecting a large, four-spoke "umbrella" of lightweight nylon and aluminum over the area where the shield had been torn away. Days later, they completed the repairwork by cutting away the metal that was pinning down the large solar panel; this enabled the panel to open.

The three teams that eventually occupied *Skylab* spent a total time in space of 171 days, with 84 of those days clocked off by the last crew. In spite of the program's shaky start, the overall mission was a tremendous success. In exhaustive medical tests, it was learned that long-term spaceflight did not appear to be detrimental to the health of the astronauts. This information could open the way for future flights to the various planets of the solar system.

In other areas of research, the *Skylab* astronauts did extensive studies of the sun, including bringing back thousands of pictures of it, and carried out a variety of experiments on crystal growing, processing of new materials, and studies on living things. They brought along space "pets"—spiders and fish—to see how weightlessness would affect their behavior. The scientific results of *Skylab* were so massive they are still being analyzed today in planning for new space experiments.

HANDSHAKE

While the Apollo moon and Skylab missions were underway, the Soviets were not idle. Because of technical problems and other reasons not well understood in the West, the Soviets gave up their race to the moon. They were in the running to the end and had even developed a spaceship capable of manned circumlunar flight. Perhaps they decided that there was no propaganda value in being second on the moon. Instead, they began to concentrate on sending robot explorers that gathered a few tiny samples at a time and returned them to earth.

A second area of Soviet concentration was the development of a manned space station. *Salyut 1* was launched on April 19, 1971, to become the first space station in orbit. It was launched more than two years before *Skylab*. After a three-man Soyuz spacecraft failed to dock with *Salyut 1*, a second Soyuz was launched, and it docked successfully with *Salyut* in June 1971. The three cosmonauts stayed in space twenty-four days before returning to earth. Their return was not a successful one, however. While still at high altitude, their capsule lost air pressure, and the three cosmonauts tragically died.

ABOVE: *SKYLAB*, SHOWING ITS REPAIRED THERMAL SHIELD AND OPENED SOLAR PANELS, IS VIEWED BY THE DEPARTING FIRST CREW.

OPP. TOP. LEFT: CREW MEMBER PAUL WEITZ ADJUSTS A BLOOD PRESSURE CUFF ON THE ARM OF JOSEPH KERWIN DURING THE FIRST MANNED *SKYLAB* MISSION.

OPP. TOP RIGHT: ASTRONAUT JACK LOUSMA PERFORMS EXTRAVEHICULAR ACTIVITY OUTSIDE THE *SKYLAB* SPACE STATION.

OPP. MIDDLE LEFT: ARABELLA, A COMMON CROSS SPIDER, SETS ABOUT SPINNING WEBS IN SPACE AS PART OF A STUDENT EXPERIMENT CONDUCTED ON BOARD *SKYLAB*.

OPP. BOTTOM LEFT: OWEN GARRIOTT ENJOYS A MEAL DURING THE SECOND MANNED SKYLAB MISSION.

OPP. BOTTOM RIGHT: CREW MEMBER CHARLES CONRAD, JR., SMILES FOLLOWING HIS HOT SHOWER ON BOARD *SKYLAB*.

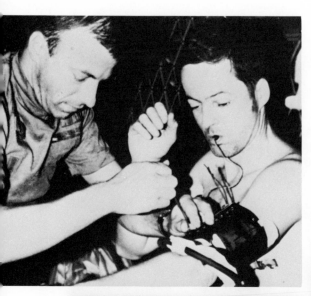

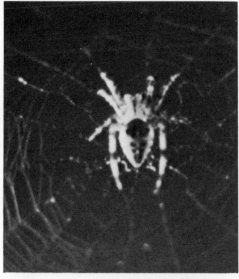

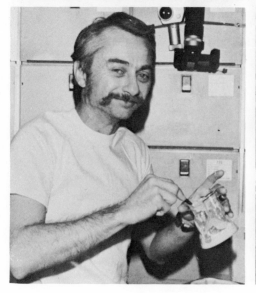

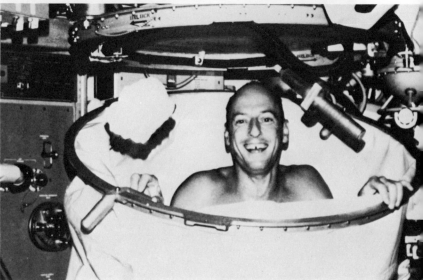

ABOVE: AN ARTIST'S DRAW-
ING OF THE HISTORIC LINKUP
OF AMERICA'S *APOLLO* WITH
THE SOVIET SOYUZ SPACE-
CRAFT IN 1975.

MIDDLE FAR LEFT: ASTRO-
NAUT DEKE SLAYTON DRIFTS
THROUGH THE DOCKING
MODULE TOWARD THE SO-
VIET SPACECRAFT DURING
THE APOLLO-SOYUZ SPACE
MISSION.

BELOW FAR LEFT: COSMO-
NAUT ALEXSEI LEONOV
IS FLANKED ON THE
RIGHT BY ASTRONAUT
TOM STAFFORD AND
ON THE LEFT BY DEKE
SLAYTON DURING THE
APOLLO-SOYUZ MISSION.

LEFT: DURING THE APOLLO-
SOYUZ SPACE MISSION,
THE APOLLO CREW TOOK
THIS UNIQUE PICTURE OF
THE SOVIET SOYUZ SPACE-
CRAFT.

In spite of the tragedy, Soviet flights continued, and in 1975 a unique space mission took place, the Apollo-Soyuz Test Project. *Soyuz 19* was launched on July 15, 1975, with Alexsei Leonov and Valeri Kubasov aboard. Seven and a half hours later, a second rocket was launched, but this one came from the United States. Tom Stafford, Deke Slayton, and Vance Brand rode in an Apollo capsule and began an around-the-world chase to rendezvous with *Soyuz.* Following docking, the hatches were opened, and the astronauts and cosmonauts shook hands in space.

For the next two days, the two craft remained linked, and the spacemen shared meals, conducted joint experiments, and flew in each other's spacecraft. Then the Soviets returned home. The Apollo crew remained in orbit for three more days.

The Apollo-Soyuz Test Project was viewed by many in the United States as a technology giveaway. One official described it as "Our arms around their shoulders and their hands in our pockets." The mission did, however, provide the United States with a rare chance to examine, close up, the state of the art of Soviet space technology.

Following the joint mission, the Soviets went on to more space station work, and in 1982, two cosmonauts spent a record 211 days in orbit. The United States, on the other hand, went into a six-year lull in manned space-flight.

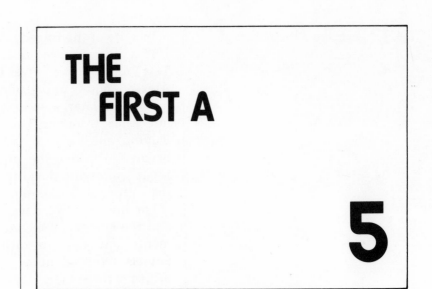

THE FIRST A

5

From the very beginning of NASA, public attention was focused squarely on space exploration. Consequently, one whole branch of aerospace work was largely ignored by the public. NASA also had the job of investigating flight through the atmosphere. That's what the first "A" in its name stands for—aeronautics.

Using research labs and some projects inherited from the old NACA, NASA continued an active aeronautics program. Studies on all types of airplanes, flying under all conditions and at various speeds, got underway.

In 1957, about the time *Sputnik* was launched, most commercial airliners were propeller driven. A year later, an event would take place that would do for aviation what *Sputnik* had done for space. In the same month that NASA was formed, the first transatlantic passenger jet service was started. In that year, for the first time, more people crossed the Atlantic by air than by ship.

NEW WINGS

One of the first important aviation developments by NASA was the invention of the variable-sweep wing. The goal was to design an airplane that could operate under many different conditions, including high-altitude, high-speed flight, and low-altitude, low-speed flight. Fixed-wing aircraft—those with the wings sticking straight out—were ideal for low-speed flight, but for high-speed flight, sweptback wings were better.

The solution was to have wings that could pivot in flight. This concept was developed both for military aircraft and for a planned supersonic transport (SST) jet for passenger flights. The SST program in the United States was canceled in 1971, however, when it became evident that technology wasn't yet up to building an economical and environmentally safe SST.

Another innovative NASA design was the supercritical airfoil. The problem that led to the creation of this design was the buildup of shock waves (the sonic boom) over the upper wing surfaces whenever an aircraft approached the speed of sound. With conventional wings, the upper surface is curved, and air travels faster over the top of the wing than under it. Even though the plane itself may not be traveling faster than the speed of sound, air flow over the wings can be; this situation produces an unstable air flow.

The solution to the problem was to build a wing with a relatively flat upper surface and a rounded under surface. This design delayed the shock wave formation and permitted the airplane to travel closer to the speed of sound without the usual vibration problems.

An even stranger wing design was the oblique, or "scissors," wing. Variable-sweep wings for aircraft are very expensive to build. In thinking about the problem, a NASA team came up with a design for a straight wing that pivots on the fuselage, like the blades of a scissor. In flight, when high-speed operation is desired, one wingtip moves forward and the other back. Pivoting the wings in this manner was far simpler than the variable-sweep concept.

POWER PLANTS

In the late 1950s, airplane fuel was cheap, and people weren't overly concerned with the environment. Then, as prices for fuel doubled and redoubled, and people became more aware of a pollution problem, NASA set about working on more efficient and less polluting ways to power aircraft. Working closely with the aviation industry, NASA began examining closely every part of a jet engine, including the inlets, fan blades, fuel injectors, and outlets. Larger diameter engines were developed that were more fuel efficient and, at the same time, produced far less noise and air pollution than previous, smaller ones had.

Though jet engines were still the primary power plant for passenger jets, NASA began reexamining the propeller. Propellers are more fuel efficient than jets, and if a way could be found to make them quieter, they might compete with jet engines. It was decided that the number of blades should be increased from three or four to eight or ten and that the blades should have broad curves. With more blades, the propellers wouldn't have to turn as fast; this, plus the curved design, would cut down on noise

LEFT: SCHEMES FOR INCREAS-
ING WING LIFT ARE TESTED
IN A FULL-SCALE WIND TUN-
NEL AT THE NASA-LANGLEY
RESEARCH CENTER.

ABOVE: A NASA TECHNICIAN
USES A LASER DEVICE TO
MEASURE THE ROTATIONAL
VELOCITY OF AN ADVANCED
PROPELLER IN A WIND TUN-
NEL TEST.

RIGHT: SPECIAL WINGS HAVE
BEEN FITTED TO THIS VARI-
ABLE-SWEEP F111, FOR TEST-
ING IN A PROGRAM CALLED
TRANSONIC AIRCRAFT TECH-
NOLOGY. BELOW THIS, A
NASA AD-1 AIRCRAFT PIVOTS
ITS WING IN FLIGHT TO
ACHIEVE INCREASED FUEL
ECONOMY. THE PIVOTAL
WING CONCEPT MAY BE USED
FOR FUTURE SUPERSONIC
AIRCRAFT.

and vibrations. Research is still continuing in this area, and it is believed that someday airplanes with new propellers might fly side-by-side with jets.

VERTICAL TAKEOFF AND LANDING (VTOL)

Another important area of aviation research was that of vertical takeoff and landing aircraft. Although helicopters can take off and land vertically, they are not very efficient for horizontal flight. Over the years, NASA, working with various branches of the military, has looked at many concepts for VTOLs. Many designs have been flown, including the Bell X14A, which has been around as a test vehicle for more than twenty years. The Bell X14A achieves vertical liftoff by aiming its jet exhaust downward. Another concept was the XC142A, which had four propellers on its wings. To fly straight up, the wings pivoted up, and to fly horizontally, they tilted forward. This aircraft had an additional propeller in the tail, for vertical flights and hovering.

The most recent VTOL is the XV-15. The wings on this aircraft remain fixed, but large rotors on the wingtips rotate for vertical or horizontal flight. Over long flights, the XV-15 has been found to be more efficient than helicopters and is able to travel much faster and quieter. This aircraft is being studied for military transports and for intercity commuter airlines.

BRIDGING AVIATION AND SPACE

In the early 1950s, a new rocket-powered aircraft was conceived that would not get its chance to fly until after NASA came into being. Three of these aircraft, designated as the X-15s, were built to investigate supersonic flight at high altitudes.

From its first flight in 1959 to its last flight in the early 1970s, the X-15 broke many altitude and speed records. Only 50 feet (16.4 m) long, with a wingspan of 22 feet (7.2 m), the X-15 was not capable of taking off from earth on its own. It was carried underneath the wing of a B-52 bomber and air-launched at 40,000 feet (13,120 m). During a flight in August 1963, pilot Joe Walker climbed to a peak altitude of more than 67 miles (107.9 km), a part of the upper atmosphere where the air was too thin to produce any effect. Control of the X-15 was accomplished by using twelve small peroxide rockets to tilt the vehicle until it

ABOVE LEFT: THE TILT-WING VERTOL 76 COMES IN FOR A LANDING IN 1960.

ABOVE RIGHT: THE XV-15 TILT-ROTOR AIRCRAFT, IN THE PROCESS OF CHANGING FROM VERTICAL TO HORIZONTAL FLIGHT, IS SHOWN HERE DURING A TEST FLIGHT. THE XV-15 COULD LEAD TO SIGNIFICANT CHANGES IN FUTURE AIR TRANSPORTATION.

MIDDLE: FOR MORE THAN TWENTY YEARS, THE BELL X-14 HAS BEEN USED BY NASA FOR INVESTIGATING VERTICAL TAKEOFF AND LANDING AIRCRAFT DESIGNS.

BELOW: THE X-15 ROCKET PLANE IS AIR-LAUNCHED FROM A B-52 DURING THIS 1960 FLIGHT.

RIGHT: AN OLD AIRFRAME IS AIMED AT THE GROUND IN A NASA ATTEMPT TO LEARN HOW TO IMPROVE SURVIVABILITY OF PASSENGERS DURING SMALL AIRCRAFT CRASHES. ROCKETS ARE USED TO INCREASE IMPACT VELOCITY. BELOW THIS, A NASA TEST PILOT INVESTIGATES FLIGHT CHARACTERISTICS BY DELIBERATELY PRODUCING STALLS AND SPINS IN THIS LIGHT AIRCRAFT. STALLS AND SPINS ARE A SIGNIFICANT SAFETY PROBLEM FOR AIRCRAFT OF THIS SIZE.

OPP. TOP: THE YF-12 AIRCRAFT HAS BEEN USED BY NASA FOR MANY YEARS TO INVESTIGATE HIGH-SPEED (GREATER THAN 2,000 MPH OR 3,220 KMPH) AND HIGH-ALTITUDE FLIGHT.

OPP. MIDDLE: THREE OF MANY LIFTING-BODY DESIGNS INVESTIGATED BY NASA AND THE U.S. AIR FORCE IN THE 1960s AND 1970s FOR POSSIBLE FUTURE SPACECRAFT DESIGNS.

OPP. BOTTOM: A REMOTELY PILOTED HiMAT (HIGHLY MANEUVERABLE AIRCRAFT TECHNOLOGY) FLIES OVER THE CALIFORNIA DESERT AT THE DRYDEN FLIGHT RESEARCH CENTER. HiMAT IS BEING EVALUATED FOR FUTURE MILITARY AIRCRAFT OF THE 1990s.

ABOVE: THE ROGALLO WING DESIGN FOR HANG GLIDING IS A DIRECT SPINOFF FROM NASA SPACECRAFT LANDING STUDIES.

RIGHT: NASA STUDIES IN 1962 OF A PARAGLIDER CONCEPT FOR RECOVERY OF SPACECRAFT EVENTUALLY LED TO THE DEVELOPMENT OF THE SPORT OF HANG GLIDING.

OPP. PAGE: WAKE VORTICES, PRODUCED BY LARGE COMMERCIAL JETS, ARE STUDIED WITH SMOKE TRAILS. VORTICES, LIKE HORIZONTAL TORNADOES, PRODUCE HAZARDS FOR SMALL AIRCRAFT TRAVELING THROUGH THE WAKE.

had dropped to a lower altitude, where the air was denser. Another X-15 record was set in 1967 when William Knight pushed his craft to a speed of more than 4,500 miles (7,245 km) per hour.

The X-15 was very helpful in developing control and insulation techniques for returning vehicles from orbit. In addition, it contributed much to our understanding of high-performance aircraft operating at supersonic speeds.

Another series of aircraft that were designed to help us solve atmospheric reentry and control problems of returning spacecraft were the so-called lifting bodies. Lifting bodies were wingless aircraft that generated lift by virtue of their body shapes. Air-launched, like the X-15, the lifting bodies flown by NASA and the Air Force contributed much to the design of the space shuttle (see pages 73 through 77).

In one lifting-body flight, pilot Bruce Peterson rode his vehicle down to a spectacular crash landing. The craft had been experiencing severe swinging motions as it approached the ground. Peterson fought to stabilize the aircraft. As he leveled out for the landing, however, a helicopter got in his way, and he tried to go beneath it. One of his landing-gear doors caught the ground, and the lifting body tumbled and bounced along the runway, kicking up a cloud of dust. Peterson somehow survived the crash. NASA films of the mishap were later acquired by television producers, and Peterson's crash landing became the introduction to the popular TV show, "The Six Million Dollar Man."

ABOVE: A BOEING 727 ROLLS THROUGH A TEST SECTION DURING RUNWAY SAFETY TESTS.

BELOW: NASA'S QUIET SHORT-HAUL RESEARCH AIRCRAFT MAKES AIRCRAFT CARRIER LANDING TESTS IN 1980.

THE UNMANNED SATELLITES

6

Just a few years after the first satellite launches, world attention became riveted on the manned space program. Satellites were all but forgotten for a while by the public.

Satellites continued to be launched with great frequency, however, as launch vehicles became more and more reliable. The first satellites were primarily designed to study the environment around the earth or were experimental devices to test systems that might be used on future satellites. Some satellites were sent into orbit around the sun.

WEATHER SATELLITES

In the early 1960s, the forerunners of the first "applications" satellites were launched. Applications satellites were built to do useful and practical jobs in space. *Tiros 1*, launched in April 1960, returned the first cloud-cover pictures of earth. It survived only two months but pointed the way to future weather satellites.

Many other Tiros satellites were launched, and toward the end of that series, a new weather satellite series, Nimbus, began. By 1964 cloud-cover maps became possible, and local weather stations were able to receive these maps directly from space. The Nimbus satellites and the more advanced weather satellites of the 1970s have greatly aided the science of weather forecasting.

COMMUNICATIONS

The first communications satellite was *Echo 1*. *Echo* was a plastic sphere, 100 feet (32.8 m) in diameter, that inflated when orbit was reached. Radio messages could be

HURRICANE ALLEN IS SHOWN
IN THIS METEOROLOGICAL
SATELLITE PICTURE TAKEN IN
AUGUST 1980. THE HURRI-
CANE COVERS NEARLY ALL
OF THE GULF OF MEXICO.

ABOVE: GROUND TESTS OF AN *ECHO* COMMUNICATIONS SATELLITE.

OPP. LEFT: THE *TELSTAR* COMMUNICATIONS SATELLITE IS BEING FITTED WITH A SHROUD FOR LAUNCH INTO SPACE.

OPP. RIGHT: *SYNCOM 1* IS BEING READIED FOR LAUNCH INTO SPACE.

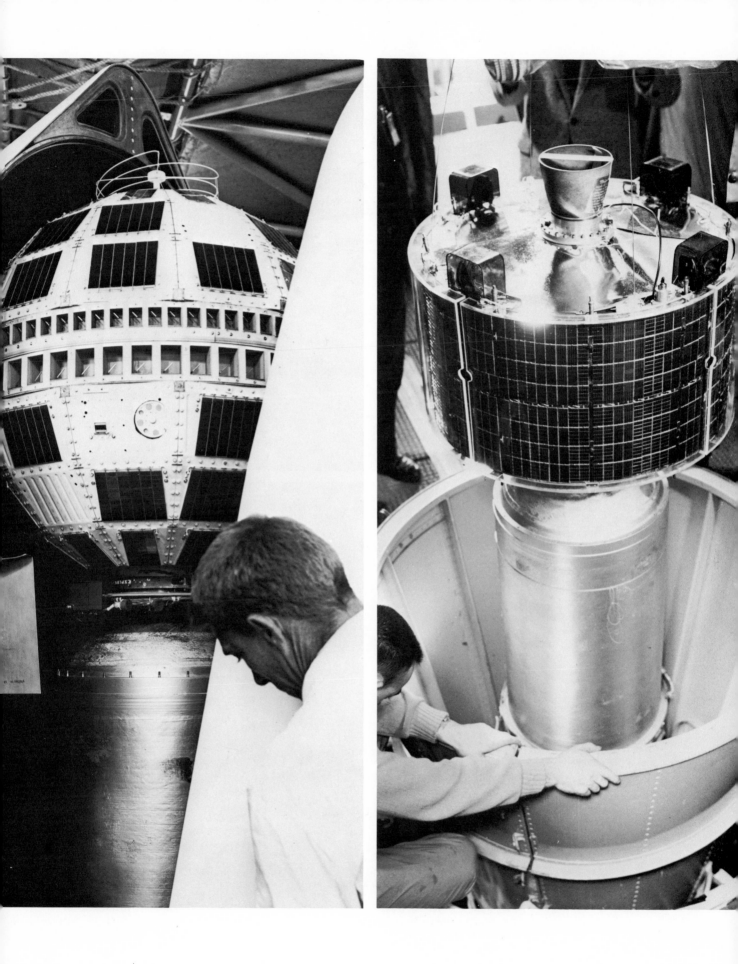

bounced off *Echo*'s metallic surface to various points on earth. Later communications satellites were more sophisticated. Transmissions to the satellites could be received, amplified, and then retransmitted to another point on earth.

Telstar 1, the first privately built satellite, gained the distinction of relaying the first television transmission from space. It was launched in July 1962. Twelve months later, *Syncom 2* became the first communications satellite to operate in geosynchronous orbit. (In this orbit, a satellite's motion can exactly parallel the rotation of the earth, keeping the satellite stationed above one point on earth. This makes geosynchronous orbit ideal for the placement of communications satellites.) Over the years, larger and more powerful communications satellites have been launched, producing a worldwide network of instantaneous communications.

LANDSAT

In 1972 a new satellite series, similar in appearance to the Nimbus satellites, was started. These satellites at first were named ERTS—Earth Resources Technology Satellites, but the name was later changed to Landsat. By 1982 four Landsats had been launched, their purpose being to gather images of the earth's land surface from space.

All four Landsats have been invaluable in the study and management of land resources on earth. Landsat images have been used to look for minerals, monitor crops and forests, study urban growth, monitor snowfall coverage and water resources, and detect pollution. Like cloud pictures from space, Landsat images are available to anyone, and scientists from more than 130 nations have put them to good use.

ABOVE: ARTIST'S CONCEPTION OF *LANDSAT* 2 IN ORBIT ABOVE THE EARTH.

BELOW: SHOWN IS A *LANDSAT* 1 PICTURE TAKEN ON SEPTEMBER 23, 1972, OF THE REGION SURROUNDING WASHINGTON, D.C. IN THIS VIEW, WATER APPEARS BLACK.

ROBOT EXPLORERS

7

While astronauts were orbiting the earth and flying to the moon, NASA was busy exploring space on another front. Venturing as far as the moon with human crews is a relatively small accomplishment when compared with the distances that have to be traversed when attempting to reach the other planets of the solar system. For those missions, NASA built robot spacecraft.

The first of these robot spacecraft to successfully complete a mission was *Mariner 2*, launched on August 27, 1962. *Mariner 1* was deliberately destroyed by NASA when its Atlas Agena rocket strayed off course. *Mariner 2* traveled for 109 days before it passed to within 22,000 miles (35,420 km) of the planet Venus. As it flew by, sensors on the craft found no magnetic field surrounding the planet and measured surface temperatures of 800°F (427°C). This was the first indication of how hot Venus really was. *Mariner 2* demonstrated the value of sending robot spacecraft to the planets for closeup observation. Peering at them through telescopes from hundreds of millions of miles away was not enough to discern their true nature.

The next Mariners were targeted at Mars. *Mariner 3* failed to work. A shroud covering the spacecraft would not jettison, and communications with the spacecraft were lost. *Mariner 4* was launched in November 1964, and in July of the next year it passed to within 6,120 miles (9,853 km) of the Red Planet. Twenty-two pictures were taken of Mars.

As *Mariner 5* was being readied for another flyby mission to Venus, other robot spacecraft were being sent to study the moon in preparation for the Apollo expeditions (see pages 22 to 25). *Mariner 5*, launched in June 1967, passed to within 4,000 miles (6,440 km) of Venus and

AN ARTIST'S DRAWING OF
THE *MARINER 2* SPACECRAFT
THAT MADE THE FIRST SUC-
CESSFUL INTERPLANETARY
MISSION.

studied the dense atmosphere. No free oxygen was found surrounding Venus, but the spacecraft did register a heavy atmosphere of carbon dioxide.

The next Mariners, 6 and 7, were launched one month apart in early 1969. They followed a more complicated course than *Mariner 4* and took fifteen and eighteen months, respectively, to make their close flybys of Mars. Again, photography was returned. All pictures, including those from *Mariner 4*, portrayed the Martian surface as a bumpy, cratered terrain that was, as one geologist put it, "uninteresting."

THE MARX BROTHERS

Though Mars seemed to be uninteresting, a major program to explore its surface was already underway. Two spacecraft, *Mariner 8* and *Mariner 9*, were designed to go into orbit around Mars, to study it and photograph its surface for a period of ninety days. *Mariner 8* failed in launch, but *Mariner 9* achieved orbit in November 1971.

As *Mariner 9* approached Mars, a giant dust storm was observed to be covering the surface of the planet. Although weather scientists were elated at the idea of being able to study weather systems on another planet, geologists were understandably upset. They couldn't see the surface, and the spacecraft might stop functioning before the storm cleared.

Gradually, the storm did clear, and, as it did, four bumps protruded through the clouds. The bumps were promptly given the unofficial nicknames of Groucho, Harpo, Chico, and Zeppo, for the Marx brothers comedy team. When all the dust had settled, the geologists were astounded. The four bumps turned out to be the tops of giant volcanoes. The largest, now named Olympus Mons, was three times the height of Mt. Everest. Other astounding discoveries were also made. A giant canyon, long enough to span the entire United States, was found, and hundreds of small channels that appeared to have been cut by running water were clearly visible. Mars was anything but uninteresting.

PLANETARY SLINGSHOT

While NASA was gearing up for an even more ambitious Mars mission, *Mariner 10* was launched toward Venus for another flyby encounter with the planet. But this time, after passing by Venus and taking photographs of the cloud patterns and readings of atmospheric pressures there, the spacecraft's course was set to take it to Mercury.

ABOVE: SEVERAL OF MARS'S GIANT VOLCANOES APPEAR AS CIRCULAR SPOTS ON THIS *VIKING 2* ORBITER VIEW OF MARS.

BELOW: MERCURY, AS SEEN IN THIS PHOTOMOSAIC MADE DURING *MARINER 10's* MARCH 29, 1974, FLYBY, SHOWS A SURFACE SIMILAR IN APPEARANCE TO THE MOON.

Mariner 10 was to take advantage of Venus's gravity and motion to propel itself in a new direction. It was as though Venus were to act as a giant slingshot.

Two months after the February 1974 Venus flyby, *Mariner 10* approached and passed by Mercury. Swinging around the sun, it made another pass at Mercury in August and a third pass in March of the following year. Photographs taken of Mercury during these passes looked very similar to those taken of the moon.

A FIRST LOOK AT JUPITER AND SATURN

It wasn't until March 1972 that a mission to the giant outer planets was attempted. Because of the great distance between the sun and Jupiter, it was felt that a spacecraft powered by solar cells wouldn't get enough sunlight to operate. To accomplish the mission, the spacecraft had to be powered with nuclear batteries. *Pioneer 10* was launched on March 2. Just a short time after its launch, it broke all speed records by topping 32,000 miles (51,520 km) per hour. It passed the moon in only eleven hours.

Following its safe passage through the asteroid belt, *Pioneer 10* flew by Jupiter in December 1973. It came to within 81,000 miles (130,410 km) of the planet's cloudtops and, while nearing Jupiter, set another speed record of 82,000 miles per hour (132,020 kmph). It took pictures of Jupiter and measured the planet's radiation and magnetic fields. After the encounter, it headed off into deep space, and by July 1979 it had crossed the orbit of Uranus. Uranus, however, was on the other side of the sun at the time.

A second Pioneer, *Pioneer 11*, followed the first into space in April 1973. It passed by Jupiter one year after *Pioneer 10*. Rather than heading into deep space, *Pioneer 11* used the slingshot effect to head across the solar system to visit Saturn in September 1979. By the time it had begun taking pictures of the Ringed Planet, *Pioneer 11* had been in space six and a half years and had traveled almost 2 billion miles (3,200 million km) through space.

LANDING ON MARS AND VOYAGER'S GRAND TOUR 8

Exactly seven years following the first manned landing on the moon, another important event took place. The *Viking 1* lander gently settled on the Chryse Basin following a parachute and rocket descent to the surface. *Viking 1* had spent three hundred days traveling to Mars and had gone into orbit several weeks prior to the landing. As the lander dropped to the surface, its sister ship, *Viking 2*, orbited high above.

Immediately following touchdown, the lander took a picture of the Martian surface. Nineteen minutes passed before the radio message, containing the encoded photograph and traveling at the speed of light, reached earth. As rocks, pebbles, sand, and one of the lander's footpads flashed onto the screen, geologists were elated. The detail was incredible. Later pictures showed the terrain for miles around the lander. Stretching out in all directions was a gently rolling landscape that was strewn with rocks and boulders of all sizes.

The first color photos of Mars showed a reddish color for all surface matter and a blue sky above. Closeup shots of the lander itself, however, revealed that these first color photos were flawed. A color chart attached to the lander did not appear as it should have. By making adjustments in a manner similar to adjusting a home TV set, the proper colors appeared. New shots of Mars were made; in these, the land appeared a rusty orange and the sky pinkish in color. Scientists theorized that the sky color was due to the tinting effect of orange dust in the wind-blown air.

Eight days after the landing, the most important Viking experiments began. A robot arm extended from the lander and scooped up soil. The samples were dropped through a funnel into a very complex science laboratory that was only 1 cubic foot (.0328 cu m) in size. Many tests were

RIGHT: A TITAN III E CENTAUR
ROCKET LIFTS OFF FROM THE
CAPE CANAVERAL AIR FORCE
STATION LAUNCH SITE ON
AUGUST 20, 1975, WITH *VIKING
1* ON BOARD.

OPP. TOP: THE HISTORIC FIRST
PHOTOGRAPH TAKEN ON THE
SURFACE OF MARS BY THE
VIKING 1 LANDER MOMENTS
AFTER IT LANDED ON JULY 20,
1976.

OPP. MIDDLE: A SPECTACULAR
LANDSCAPE PICTURE OF THE
SURFACE OF MARS, REVEAL-
ING ROCKS AND SAND
DUNES, WAS TAKEN BY THE
VIKING 1 LANDER ON AUGUST
4, 1976.

OPP. BOTTOM: THE GIANT
MARTIAN VOLCANO, OLYM-
PUS MONS, IS SHOWN IN THIS
VIKING 1 ORBITER PICTURE
TAKEN FROM A DISTANCE OF
ABOUT 5,000 MILES (8,050 KM)
ON JULY 31, 1976.

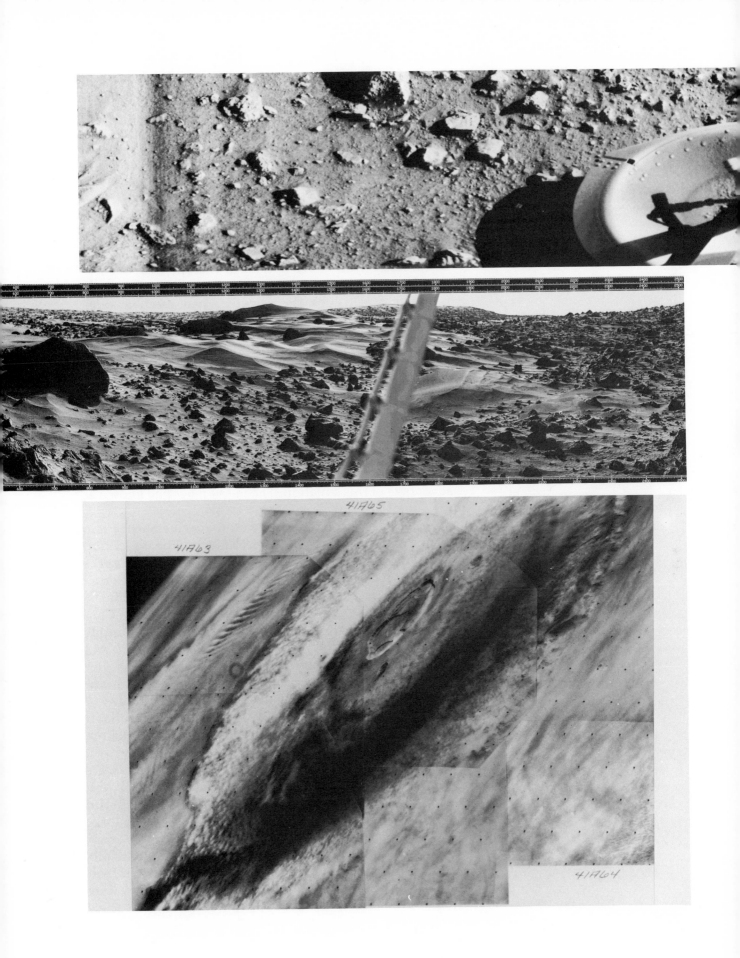

conducted on the samples to try to determine if living organisms were present in the soil. As the first data was returned to earth, it seemed as if life were present on Mars. Something in the soil seemed to be eating, breathing, and growing. But other experiments on the lander were giving conflicting evidence. The scientists cautiously concluded that some unusual chemical reactions that partially simulated the effects of living organisms were taking place.

In September, the second Viking lander separated from its orbiting spacecraft and touched down in the Utopia Basin. Rocks were more numerous there than at the first site, but life-science experiments confirmed the disappointing conclusions the scientists had reached about Martian life.

THE GRAND TOUR

Once every 175 years, the giant planets line up in their orbits around the sun in such a way that permits a spacecraft from earth to visit each of them on a single flight. Passing by Jupiter first, that planet's gravity bends the spacecraft's fightpath toward Saturn, and so on. A NASA mission was proposed in the late 1960s to take advantage of this situation. The mission became known as the Grand Tour.

To build a spacecraft that would survive such a trip would require much new technology. The spacecraft would have to operate in the deadly environment of space for more than ten years, be able to perform complicated maneuvers, and be able to run itself for long periods.

Although the Grand Tour was never funded by Congress, a mini-tour to Jupiter and Saturn was. Two durable spacecraft, named *Voyager 1* and *Voyager 2*, were built and launched in 1977. *Voyager 1* was launched two weeks after *Voyager 2* but traveled a faster course and arrived at Jupiter first, in March 1979. Four months later, *Voyager 2* arrived. Pictures sent back by the two spacecraft astounded the world. A ring around Jupiter was discovered. Jupiter's moon Io was found to have giant active volcanoes spewing out sulfur compounds. Other moons were found to be icy, rocky balls with fractures and craters. Time lapse motion pictures were made of the colorful swirling of the gases around the planet.

After *Voyager 1* left Jupiter, it headed for Saturn. *Voyager 2* followed. Again the world was astounded by the pictures sent back during the 1980 and 1981 encounters. Saturn's rings, once thought to total three or four, were found to consist of thousands of concentric ringlets. New

VOYAGER 1 TOOK THIS SPEC-
TACULAR PHOTO OF JUPITER
ON FEBRUARY 13, 1979, WHEN
THE SPACECRAFT WAS MORE
THAN 12 MILLION MILES
(19.3 MILLION KM) FROM THE
PLANET. THE MOON IO IS IN
FRONT OF JUPITER'S GREAT
RED SPOT, AND EUROPA IS
OFF TO THE RIGHT.

ABOVE: IN 1978, WHILE THE GRAND TOUR WAS IN FULL-SWING, NASA UNDERTOOK ANOTHER MISSION TO VENUS. THIS PHOTOGRAPH WAS TAKEN BY A *PIONEER VENUS ORBITER* IN MARCH 1979.

OPP. TOP: SATURN, AS RECORDED BY *VOYAGER 2* FROM A DISTANCE OF 13 MILLION MILES (20.9 MILLION KM) ON AUGUST 4, 1981. THREE OF SATURN'S MOONS, TETHYS, DIONE, AND RHEA, ARE VISIBLE AS WHITE SPOTS, AND TETHYS' SHADOW APPEARS ON SATURN.

OPP. BOTTOM: GREAT COMPLEXITY IN SATURN'S RINGS WAS DISCOVERED BY THE TWO VOYAGER SPACECRAFT. THIS *VOYAGER 2* IMAGE WAS TAKEN FROM 5.5 MILLION MILES (8.9 MILLION KM) AWAY ON AUGUST 17, 1981.

moons were discovered, and previously known moons were seen for the first time.

Following the encounter with Saturn, *Voyager 1* headed out of the solar system, in a different direction from *Pioneer 10* and *Pioneer 11*. It began a trip to the stars that would take tens of thousands of years before even the nearest star would be reached. *Voyager 2*, however, was targeted for an encounter with Uranus in 1986 and Neptune in 1989. If still working by then, *Voyager 2* will have visited all the giant planets, and the mini-tour will have become the Grand Tour after all.

BACK TO VENUS

While the United States was concentrating its efforts on Mars and the outer planets, the Soviets were involved in an extensive program to study Venus. Eventually, they soft-landed four spacecraft there that were able to transmit a few pictures of Venus's surface back to earth.

In 1978 NASA undertook another mission to Venus. This one involved two Pioneer spacecraft—an orbiter and a multiprobe. The orbiter arrived in the vicinity of Venus on December 4, 1978, just five days before the multiprobe. It swung into orbit and set about photographing cloud patterns and bouncing radar off the surface in order to make rough maps of the terrain.

Weeks before the multiprobe arrived, it had split into five parts. Each part was designed to penetrate the atmosphere intact and take measurements while dropping to the surface. On their torturous descent, the probes passed through several different atmospheric layers, including one filled with lightning discharges. Eventually, the probes failed in the intense heat and pressure of the atmosphere. Meanwhile, the orbiter was mapping high mountains, deep valleys, and continentlike landmasses.

THE FIRST TRUE SPACESHIP

9

While astronauts John Young and Charles Duke were busy collecting more than 200 pounds (90.9 kg) of lunar samples during the *Apollo 16* mission in 1972, Mission Control radioed exciting news to the explorers. Congress had just approved money to develop the space shuttle. The shuttle would be the world's first true spaceship. Unlike all previous space-launch vehicles, which were thrown away after just one use, the shuttle would be used over and over again. The obvious advantage to this was cost. It would be much cheaper to operate than conventional rockets of the same payload size. Furthermore, it would be more versatile and could be made ready for return to space with a minimum turnaround time on the ground.

Though the exact design of the shuttle hadn't been determined, it was decided that it would basically be a four-piece launch vehicle. The main part would be a delta-winged orbiter that would travel into space as a rocket, operate in orbit as a spacecraft, and return to earth as an airplane. Fuel for the orbiter's engines would come from a large strap-on tank; attached to this would be two solid rocket boosters.

It was appropriate that Young was in space when approval for the shuttle came through. Almost nine years to the day after he heard the news, Young would become the commander of the first shuttle test flight in space.

SHUTTLE TAKES SHAPE

In the years following Apollo, the shuttle began to take shape. The orbiter would be 122 feet (40 m) long, which, ironically, was just slightly longer than the distance first flown by the Wright brothers in 1903. The wingspan of the orbiter would be 78 feet (25.6 m), and the back of the craft would be split down the middle by two clamshell doors that, when open, would reveal a payload bay 60 feet (19.6 m) long and 15 feet (4.9 m) in diameter. The nose of the orbiter would house two main decks, one for the flight and payload-bay controls and the other for living quarters and storage.

The external fuel tank for the orbiter's three main engines turned out to look like a farm silo, but with a rounded base. It would disintegrate in the atmosphere after it was discarded. The boosters, on the other hand, would make it back to earth, with parachutes to slow their fall into the Atlantic and ships waiting nearby to tow them back to shore.

APPROACH AND LANDING TESTS

One of the most critical phases in the proposed flight of the shuttle was its gliderlike landing on earth. For normal airplanes, this would not have been a problem, but to survive reentry into the atmosphere, the shuttle's wings had to be small without sacrificing stability and glide. Computer simulations and model tests showed that the orbiter could safely glide to earth, but the most important test was still to come.

The first shuttle orbiter to be constructed, the *Enterprise,* was prepared for drop tests at the Dryden Flight Research Center in California. To lift the orbiter above the ground, a 747 jet was modified, and the *Enterprise* was placed on its back.

On August 12, 1977, the piggybacked *Enterprise* was carried to an altitude of 21,800 feet (7,150 m). The 747 then went into a shallow dive, and the *Enterprise* was cut loose from the top. It took the *Enterprise* and its crew of two astronauts five and a half minutes to glide to the ground. The landing was smooth and precise. Three more flights were made that year, and the results were all excellent.

TROUBLES

Not all work on the shuttle proceeded smoothly, however. The main engines of the orbiter were the most powerful of their size ever designed. Because of friction, improper welding materials, and a number of other causes, the engines failed, and some even exploded during tests. Furthermore, the heat-shield system, consisting of silica tiles that looked like bricks and were glued to the

ABOVE: AN EARLY (1969) NASA CONCEPT OF A SPACE SHUTTLE SPACE VEHICLE.

BELOW: THE SPACE SHUTTLE *ENTERPRISE* SEPARATES FROM ITS CARRIER AIRCRAFT DURING AN APPROACH-AND-LANDING TEST ON OCTOBER 12, 1977.

orbiter's exterior, were not bonding properly. These and other problems slowed down the shuttle's development.

Actually, the situation was not as bleak as it seemed to many. The public had forgotten how difficult it had been to launch the first space missions. The shuttle would be the most complicated flying machine ever constructed, and development difficulties were to be expected.

One result of the delay in the shuttle was most saddening. The first flights were planned for the late 1970s. About that time, *Skylab* was expected to reenter the atmosphere. It was hoped that the shuttle would be ready in time to rescue *Skylab* by attaching a rocket to it and boosting it to a higher orbit. However, the shuttle was not ready when, in July 1979, *Skylab* made its fiery reentry. Back in 1962, when John Glenn had orbited the earth, the citizens of Perth, Australia, had turned on every light possible to signal a friendly hello to Glenn through the darkness. *Skylab* returned the favor by lighting up the sky over Perth fifteen years later.

A SPACE TRANSPORTATION SYSTEM (STS) IS BORN

A computer timing problem forced a two-day delay of the first shuttle test flight. On April 12, 1981, by chance the twentieth anniversary of the historic flight of Yuri Gagarin, the shuttle flew for the first time. Just after sunrise, the space shuttle *Columbia*, on mission STS-1, thundered off the same launch complex that was used for the Apollo moon expeditions. The sunlike flames of the boosters stretched out more than three times the length of the vehicle—almost 700 feet (230 m). Rising on a pillar of smoke and fire, the *Columbia*, with astronauts John Young and Robert Crippen aboard, opened a new era in space travel.

At two minutes and ten seconds into the flight, the boosters separated and then fell into the ocean for recovery. Six and a half minutes later, the external tank ran dry and was ejected. It disintegrated over the Indian Ocean. The *Columbia* continued to climb, using the power of its two orbital maneuvering system (OMS) engines.

During the fifty-four hour mission, Young and Crippen opened the payload-bay doors and tested many onboard systems. A few of the heat-shield tiles had fallen off, but none in critical areas.

The OMS engines fired again, this time in the opposite direction from the motion of the orbiter, and *Columbia* started its reentry. A half hour later, observers at Dryden Air Force Base in California heard a double sonic boom.

ABOVE LEFT: THE SPACE SHUTTLE *COLUMBIA* BEGINS ITS FIRST TEST FLIGHT INTO SPACE. THE FLIGHT LASTED FIFTY-FOUR HOURS.

ABOVE RIGHT: THE CREW OF THE FIRST SPACE SHUTTLE TEST FLIGHT, MISSION COMMANDER JOHN YOUNG (*LEFT*) AND BOB CRIPPEN (*RIGHT*), GIVE THE "THUMBS UP" SIGN DURING A PREFLIGHT SIMULATION.

BELOW: THE SPACE SHUTTLE *COLUMBIA* LANDS ON A DRY LAKEBED AT EDWARDS AIR FORCE BASE IN CALIFORNIA FOLLOWING ITS FIRST TEST FLIGHT INTO SPACE.

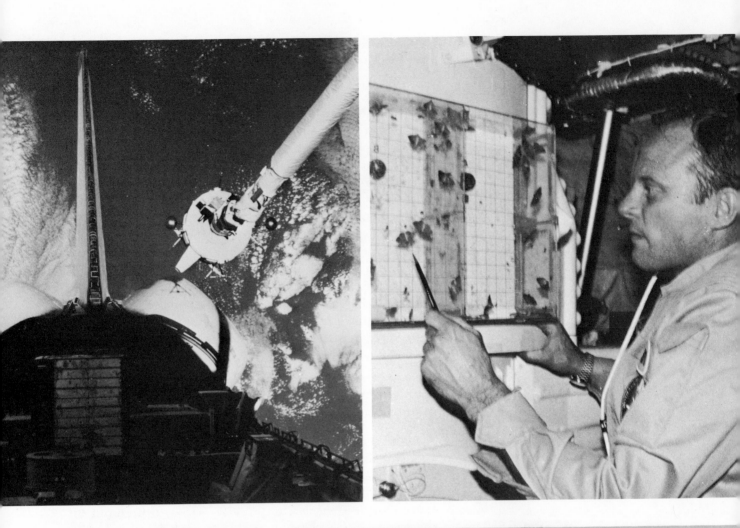

ABOVE: A PACKAGE OF EXPER-
IMENTS IS "WAVED" ABOUT
THE OPEN PAYLOAD BAY OF
COLUMBIA BY THE ORBITER'S
ROBOT ARM DURING THE STS-
3 MISSION.

ABOVE RIGHT: ASTRONAUT
JACK LOUSMA EXAMINES
SOME MOTHS, BEES, AND
HOUSEFLIES IN A STUDENT
EXPERIMENT CARRIED
ALOFT DURING STS-3.

RIGHT: THE LAUNCHPAD AND
SERVICE STRUCTURES ARE
CLEARLY VISIBLE AS THE
FINAL PREPARATIONS ARE
MADE FOR *COLUMBIA*'S FIRST
OPERATIONAL SPACEFLIGHT
ON NOVEMBER 11, 1982.

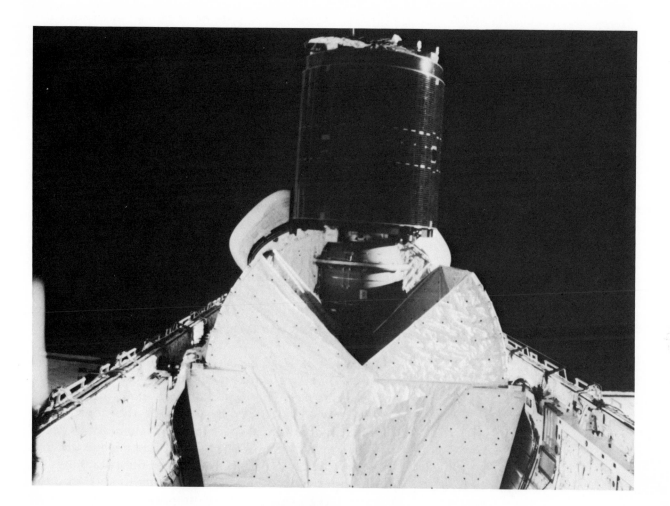

ABOVE: SBS-3, THE FIRST SAT-
ELLITE TO BE LAUNCHED
FROM THE SPACE SHUTTLE, IS
SPRING-EJECTED FROM THE
PAYLOAD BAY OF *COLUMBIA*.

RIGHT: FOLLOWING THEIR
SUCCESSFUL DEPLOYMENT
OF TWO COMMUNICATIONS
SATELLITES, THE CREW OF
COLUMBIA'S FIFTH FLIGHT
PROUDLY ADVERTISE THEIR
SERVICE. STARTING WITH
MISSION COMMANDER
VANCE BRAND (IN BLACK
SHIRT) AND GOING CLOCK-
WISE, THEY ARE: WILLIAM
LENOIR (MISSION SPECIAL-
IST), BOB OVERMYER (PILOT),
AND JOE ALLEN (MISSION
SPECIALIST).

Minutes later, *Columbia* touched down on Runway 23 on the Rogers dry lakebed.

STS-2 TO 4

Over the next fifteen months, the *Columbia* was flown in three more test flights. The second mission demonstrated that the space shuttle was reusable, and that a 50-foot-long (16.4-m) robot arm it carried did indeed work. The mission was shortened because of fuel-cell problems.

The third mission carried a payload of scientific instruments, as did the second, but the robot arm was used to pick up one of the instruments and wave it above the bay to make electric field measurements. This mission was lengthened from seven to eight days. Because rain had soaked the lakebed runway at Dryden, turning it into mud, the landing had to be shifted to White Sands, New Mexico. But high winds there forced the one-day landing delay.

On July 4, 1982, *Columbia* made its fourth return from space. A classified Department of Defense payload was carried in its bay. The important fact about this mission, however, was that after it was over the shuttle was declared an operational space launch system. It was ready to do the jobs it was designed to do. One mishap did mar the nearly perfect mission. Failures of the parachutes on both booster rockets caused the rockets to sink into the Atlantic Ocean, making them impossible to recover or reuse.

OPERATIONAL STATUS

The first operational flight of the space shuttle began on November 11, 1982. For the first time, four astronauts were on board a single launch vehicle. Two of the astronauts were mission specialists, and it was their job to see that two privately owned communications satellites were properly launched.

Six hours after liftoff, the first satellite was spun to provide stability and spring-ejected from the payload bay. Exactly forty-five minutes later, a rocket attached to the satellite fired, sending it into geosynchronous orbit. The second satellite was launched in an identical manner a day later.

Columbia's return five days later had to be switched from the dirt runway at Dryden to a concrete runway. For the second time in the first five flights of *Columbia*, it had rained in the desert.

THINGS TO COME

10

A quarter of a century has passed since the first satellites were launched into orbit. During that time, human beings have made their first tentative probings into the harsh world of interplanetary space. We have walked on the moon. Robot spacecraft have traveled to planets as far out as Saturn. Networks of satellites now girdle the earth, and new and sometimes strange-looking airplanes have taken to the air. It has been an exciting and challenging time for NASA, with some failures but many successes.

The next twenty-five years—will they be as exciting and as challenging? What can we expect to see? Let's take a look at just a few of the things to come.

In the next few years, four space shuttle orbiters will be ready for service, and two launch and landing sites will be in operation. Most flights will continue to take off and land at the Kennedy Space Center in Florida, but others will originate at the Vandenberg Air Force Base in California. With two launch sites and four orbiters, there may be a new flight into space every week or two.

On the missions to come, shuttles will carry all kinds of payloads into space. New satellites will be launched—some so big that they will have to be assembled in orbit from parts brought up by one or more shuttles. Communications satellites will be larger and more powerful, so that people will be able to use wrist telephones to talk to anyone anywhere in the world.

Science laboratories such as the European Space Agency's Spacelab, designed for the shuttle's payload bay, will be flown repeatedly. These will be the forerunners of space factories that will manufacture new materials and medicines in space. A new label—Made in Space—should begin to appear on products in stores.

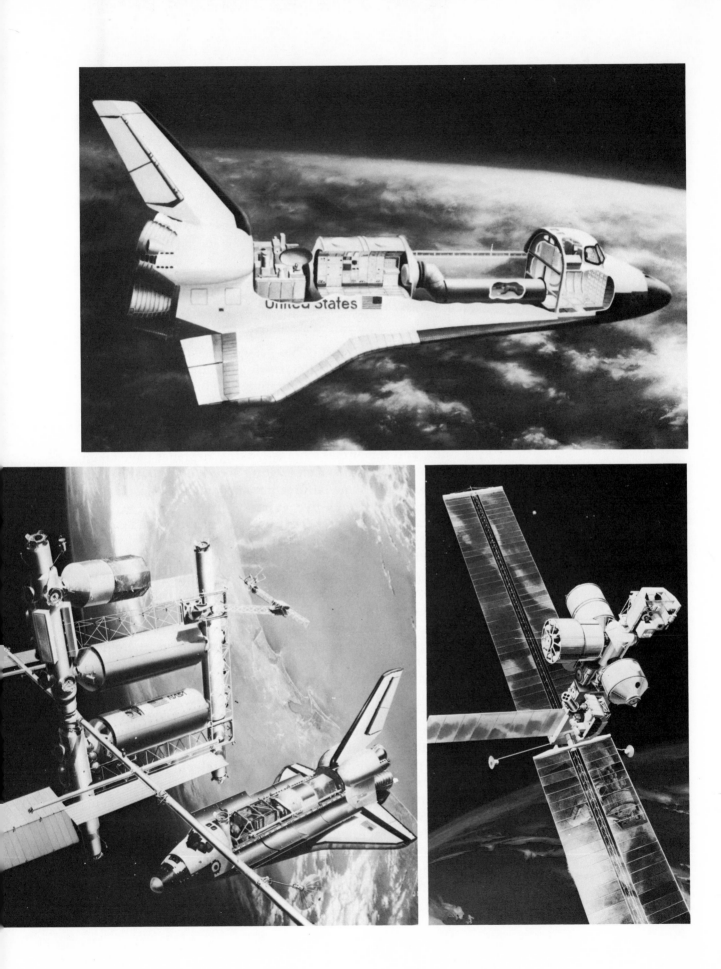

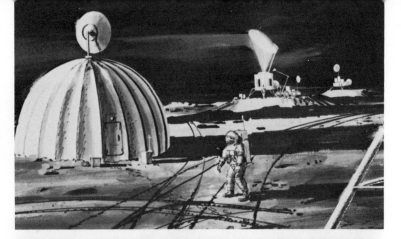

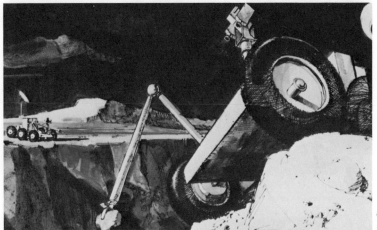

OPP. TOP: THIS IS AN ARTIST'S CONCEPTION OF THE 1983 *SPACELAB 1* MISSION. THE CUTAWAY VIEW SHOWS HOW CREW MEMBERS WILL ENTER THE CYLINDRICAL LABORATORY FROM THE MID-DECK IN THE SHUTTLE'S NOSE.

OPP. BOTTOM LEFT: THE SPACE OPERATIONS CENTER (SOC) IS ONE OF SEVERAL SPACE STATION CONCEPTS NASA IS STUDYING. THE CYLINDRICAL MODULES OF THE STATION HOUSE CREW MEMBERS, WHOSE JOBS WOULD BE TO SERVICE SATELLITES, CONDUCT EXPERIMENTS, AND STUDY EARTH FROM SPACE.

OPP. BOTTOM RIGHT: ANOTHER VERSION OF A POSSIBLE SPACE STATION IS THIS MODULAR SPACE PLATFORM. THE LARGE, FLAT PANELS TO THE SIDE CAPTURE SOLAR ENERGY TO POWER THE STATION. THE VERTICAL PANEL SERVES AS A HEAT RADIATOR.

ABOVE RIGHT: AN ARTIST'S CONCEPTION OF A FUTURE LUNAR BASE.

MIDDLE: CONCEPTION FOR A ROBOT-ROVING VEHICLE FOR EXPLORING MARS.

RIGHT: THE SPACE TELESCOPE IS SHOWN HERE AS IT IS EXPECTED TO LOOK WHEN LAUNCHED IN 1985 OR 1986. THE UNOBSTRUCTED VIEW FROM SPACE SHOULD PERMIT THE SPACE TELESCOPE TO PEER SEVEN TIMES DEEPER INTO SPACE THAN IS POSSIBLE WITH GROUND-BASED TELESCOPES.

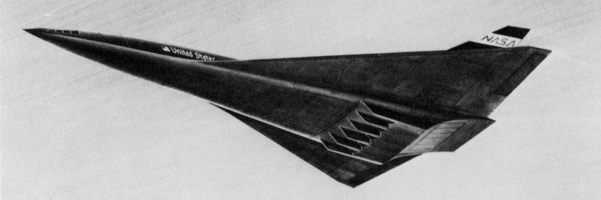

TOP: A LARGE, MULTIBODY TRANSPORT AIRCRAFT CONCEPT IS BEING STUDIED AS A METHOD OF REDUCING COSTS IN AIR SHIPMENT OF CARGO.

ABOVE: SHOWN HERE IS ONE OF MANY DESIGNS FOR FUTURE PASSENGER AIRCRAFT. THIS AIRLINER MIGHT BE CAPABLE OF CRUISING AT 4,000 MPH (6,440 KMPH).

RIGHT: A "RING WING" CONCEPT FOR AIRPLANES IS BEING LOOKED AT FOR THE POST-2000 TIME PERIOD.

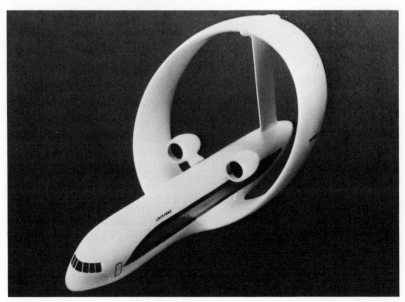

Temporary science laboratories will pave the way for more permanent facilities for scientists to work in space. Large cylindrical modules may be carried into space by the shuttle and assembled into space stations. With enough modules joined together, a permanent habitat will be possible, permitting astronauts to live and work for months in space before coming down to earth for vacations. The station crews may be assigned to satellite servicing and repair, assembly and launch of interplanetary spacecraft, scientific research, or earth-monitoring tasks.

The next twenty-five years may even see the beginnings of the first permanent scientific facilities on the moon and Mars. These could eventually grow into small cities. During that time, the first human babies may be born on another world.

Along with an increase in human spaceflight will be the continued exploration of the solar system. *Voyager 2* will fly by Uranus in 1986 and by Neptune in 1989. A new spacecraft mission, called Galileo, is being planned to send a probe into Jupiter's atmosphere, while another spacecraft may produce radar maps of Venus and still others might land on the larger moons of Jupiter and Saturn. Robot cars may roam around on the surface of Mars. Furthermore, it is hoped that by 1985 the Space Telescope will be in orbit above the earth. This telescope's large mirror system will probe seven times deeper into the universe than is now possible with earth-based telescopes.

Back on earth, satellites will help people take better care of their world. Satellite observations will help us protect crops from disease, manage agricultural, forest, and water resources, and control pollution.

Travel through the atmosphere will improve, as airplanes are built that will fly farther on less fuel and create less noise and pollution. Large commuter planes will be able to take off and land vertically from the middle of cities, thus serving people more effectively than is usually possible now.

Forecasts for the future, such as these, are always subject to overstatement. What actually takes place may be entirely different. Yet the National Aeronautics and Space Administration is working with industry, universities, and other governmental agencies on many of these ideas right now or is developing the technology that could lead to them. While these forecasts may seem wild and impossible to some, to others they do not. People like Wilbur and Orville Wright, Robert Goddard, Wernher von Braun, and Neil Armstrong thrived on ideas like these. It is the stuff that made up their lives. If you were to ask any of these aerospace pioneers what they thought of today's forecasts, they would probably reply, "Let's get started!"

FOR FURTHER READING

Many fine books on the programs and accomplishments of the National Aeronautics and Space Administration are available in libraries. In addition, NASA itself has published a number of pamphlets and books on its work, and the more recent ones are available in libraries or from the Superintendent of Documents, U.S. Government Printing Office, Washington, DC 20402. A list of these publications is given below. Contact the GPO for current prices.

EP-57 Man in Space. A chronicle of the Mercury, Gemini, and Apollo manned spaceflight programs. 1969. Stock No. 033-000-00155-0.

EP-85 NASA Aeronautics. A colorful book on NASA's aeronautical research and development, telling about the aircraft being developed that will fly in the 1980s. 1980. Stock No. 033-000-00796-5.

EP-100 Apollo. A commemorative book summarizing the historic manned lunar-landing program, with some of the best color photographs from each Apollo mission. 1974. Stock No. 033-000-00553-9.

EP-109 Apollo-Soyuz. The story of the historic Apollo-Soyuz Test Project. 1977. Stock No. 033-000-00652-7.

EP-131 What's New on the Moon? This book summarizes new knowledge obtained through the Apollo expeditions to the moon. 1976. Stock No. 033-000-00653-5.

EP-145 Sixty Years of Aeronautical Research. 1917–1977. The story of the contribution of NASA's Langley Research Center to air and space flight. 1980. Stock No. 033-000-00745-1.

EP-146 *Mars: The Viking Discoveries.* Color and black-and-white photographs from the Viking landers and orbiters illustrate this booklet, which features results of the Viking mission to Mars. 1977. Stock No. 033-000-00703-5.

EP-156 *The Space Shuttle at Work.* Describes the space shuttle and its potential for serving programs of the future. 1979. Stock No. 033-000-00779-5.

EP-169 *Aboard the Space Shuttle.* This fascinating, full-color booklet tells you what it is like to be aboard the space shuttle. 1980. Stock No. 033-000-00806-6.

EP-177 *A Meeting with the Universe.* This beautifully illustrated book is the story of what we have learned about the universe and ourselves by going into space. 1982. Stock No. 033-000-00836-8.

EP-191 *The Voyager Flights to Jupiter and Saturn.* A well-illustrated color booklet filled with spectacular photographs of Jupiter and Saturn taken by the Voyager spacecraft. 1982. Stock No. 033-000-00854-6.

SP-350 *Apollo Expeditions to the Moon.* A history of the Apollo program as told by the Apollo astronauts and top NASA executives. 1975. Stock No. 033-000-00630-6.

SP-360 *Mission to Earth: Landsat Views the World.* A compendium of outstanding Landsat scenes in full color, depicting the earth's surface from a perspective never before presented in such breadth and detail. 1977. Stock No. 033-000-00659-4.

INDEX